"Forget what you think you know about assertiveness and read this book! It's given me a much better understanding of what assertiveness truly is and helped me strengthen my relationships and communication in all areas of my life."

David Philhower
Insurance Underwriter
Raleigh, North Carolina

"*Caring Assertiveness* has helped me to have more effective conversations with my patients—especially those difficult conversations a physician sometimes needs to have. The skills it offers should be taught in medical school."

Deanna Carr, M.D.
Physician
Ocoee, Florida

"As an airline pilot, reading *Caring Assertiveness* has helped me improve my communication skills with crew, dispatchers, ground personnel, passengers, and beyond. Assertive relating eliminates the barriers that sometimes surround airline captains, helping me develop positive professional relationships and become a kinder, gentler person."

Dale Heitshusen
Commercial Airline Pilot
Dallas, Texas

"Reading *Caring Assertiveness* and learning how to respect both myself and others at the same time was very freeing. It's so well written, with concrete techniques that guide you in communicating more assertively. I can't stop thinking of people I want to give this book to."

Janel Cooper
Lead Emergency Dispatcher
St. Louis, Missouri

"*Caring Assertiveness* is filled with highly practical information and illustrations that show how to be truly assertive. This is a much-needed book in today's world."

Carlos Velazquez, Ph.D.
Clinical Psychologist
Canóvanas, Puerto Rico

"Many books tell you *what to do* without telling you *how*. **Caring Assertiveness** also gives you the *how*. It's so full of great, usable ideas that I was highlighting and underlining all the way through."

Talita Grayton
Operations Specialist
Washington, D.C.

"I believe any pastor—and any church—would benefit from **Caring Assertiveness**. The book's examples of how Jesus lived assertively and its examination of human emotions are invaluable, connecting directly to real life. A wonderful resource!"

Rev. Gale Tien
Pastor
Jenison, Michigan

"This book is life-changing! It helped me hone my interpersonal skills and gave me concrete ideas for becoming more assertive. It's an indispensable tool for better relating with family, friends, clients, coworkers, and others—a must-read!"

Sally Cancilla
Fitness Instructor
Toronto, Ontario

"Once I started reading **Caring Assertiveness**, I couldn't put it down. I just kept turning the pages, discovering new ideas, and finding ways to improve my relationships! The book is written in such an easy-to-follow, easy-to-understand way that I couldn't help but learn from it."

Lee Mason
Business Executive
Gilbert, Arizona

"**Caring Assertiveness** is an amazing resource that's perfect for all of us. It explains how to be assertive in all kinds of situations and relationships—marriage, parenting, friendship, and in the workplace. Read it and benefit in every aspect of life!"

Janine Hunt
Nonprofit Cofounder
Bonney Lake, Washington

Caring Assertiveness

Relating Directly,
Honestly, and with Respect

ALSO FROM STEPHEN MINISTRIES

The Gift of Empathy: Helping Others Feel Valued, Cared for, and Understood

Journeying through Grief:
- **Book 1:** *A Time to Grieve*
- **Book 2:** *Experiencing Grief*
- **Book 3:** *Finding Hope and Healing*
- **Book 4:** *Rebuilding and Remembering*

Don't Sing Songs to a Heavy Heart: How to Relate to Those Who Are Suffering

Christian Caregiving—a Way of Life

Joy Comes with the Morning, Devotional Edition

Discovering God's Vision for Your Life: You and Your Spiritual Gifts

Cancer—Now What? Taking Action, Finding Hope, and Navigating the Journey Ahead

Caring Assertiveness

Relating Directly,
Honestly, and with Respect

Kenneth C. Haugk
Joel P. Bretscher
Robert A. Musser

Stephen Ministries • St. Louis, Missouri

Caring Assertiveness
Relating Directly, Honestly, and with Respect

Copyright © 2024 by Stephen Ministries St. Louis. All rights reserved.

ISBN: 978-1-930445-13-0

Library of Congress Control Number: 2024936317

All Scripture quotations, unless otherwise noted, are from the Holy Bible, NEW INTERNATIONAL VERSION®, NIV®. Copyright © 1973, 1978, 1984, 2011 by Biblica, Inc.™ Used by permission. All rights reserved worldwide.

Scripture quotations marked ESV are from the Holy Bible, English Standard Version, copyright © 2001 by Crossway Bibles, a publishing ministry of Good News Publishers.

Scripture quotations marked NKJV are from the Holy Bible, New King James Version. Copyright © 1982 by Thomas Nelson. Used by permission. All rights reserved.

No portion of this publication may be reproduced, stored in a retrieval system, or transmitted in any form or by any means—whether electronic, mechanical, photocopying, recording, or otherwise—except for brief quotations in articles or reviews, without the prior written permission of the publisher. For permission, write to:

> Stephen Ministries Permissions Department
> 2045 Innerbelt Business Center Drive
> St. Louis, Missouri 63114-5765
> (314) 428-2600

Printed in the USA

To a world in great need
of direct, honest, and
respectful relating

CONTENTS

Introduction: Assertiveness Is Caring 1

PART 1: What Is Assertiveness?

1 | A Journey Worth Taking................................ 7

2 | Passive, Aggressive, and Assertive..................... 12

3 | Benefits of Assertiveness 23

4 | What to *Say* When You Want to Be Assertive 35

5 | What to *Do* When You Want to Be Assertive 45

PART 2: Assertiveness Skills in Everyday Life

6 | Making and Responding to Requests 53

7 | Giving and Receiving Feedback........................ 66

8 | Offering, Asking for, and Accepting Help.............. 79

9 | Expressing and Receiving Anger....................... 91

10 | Giving and Responding to Compliments
     and Appreciation................................... 107

11 | Assertively Choosing to Act Passively
     or Aggressively.................................... 116

PART 3: A Faith Perspective on Assertiveness

A Note about Part 3 124

12 | Jesus as a Model of Assertiveness 125

13 | From Misunderstanding to Understanding 140

14 | Relating Assertively to God....................... 150

CONTENTS

PART 4: Taking Assertiveness to the Next Level

15 | Assertive Listening 167

16 | Assertiveness in Challenging Situations 172

17 | The Caring Candor Window 179

18 | Continuing the Journey 187

Acknowledgments 193

About the Authors 196

About the *Caring Assertiveness Discussion Guide* 198

INTRODUCTION
Assertiveness Is Caring

Assertiveness is caring. When you relate to others assertively, you show them genuine care.

This may come as a surprise to some. There's a common belief that care and assertiveness don't mix—that you have to choose one or the other. People may say that assertiveness means being tough with someone, relating bluntly and doing whatever it takes to get what you want. Or, they may argue that to be caring means weakening everything you say and focusing on other people's needs, not your own.

Neither of those beliefs is true. Bulldozing over others to get your own way is aggression, and ignoring yourself and your own needs is passivity. Both approaches are about as far from assertiveness as you can get.

In fact, relating assertively is all about caring.

- It means caring for the *other person* by speaking to them honestly, treating them with respect.
- It means caring for *yourself* by communicating directly and clearly your own thoughts, feelings, wants, and needs.

INTRODUCTION

- It may also mean caring for *others* by speaking up for them when the need arises.

This book will go into greater detail about what assertiveness is and how it works, but simply put, assertiveness involves relating *directly, honestly,* and *with respect.*

- Relating *directly* communicates clearly without leaving the other person confused or uncertain. That's a caring way to express what's on your mind.

- Relating *honestly* shares what you really think and feel, not deceiving others or hiding your true meaning. Telling the truth is key to healthy communication, and it's an act of care.

- Relating *with respect* shows that you view the person you're talking with as having real value. Respect is at the heart of your assertiveness.

We sought to put assertiveness into practice throughout the writing of this book. With every round of writing, editing, and refining, we kept assertiveness at the foundation of our work together. We made it a priority to communicate our thoughts with clarity, candor, and mutual respect while seeking to understand one another.

Assertiveness was also important as we went about conducting our research. Through focus groups, interviews, and surveys, we connected with more than 4,000 people, learning about their experiences and gathering their thoughts and ideas on various facets of assertive relating. Many of the stories and examples throughout this book are based on what they shared with us.

> When you relate to others assertively, you show them genuine care.

Another 414 individuals read and reviewed the entire manuscript before publication. Throughout this process, we encouraged each person to be completely open and honest about any feedback, opinions, thoughts, or experiences. We carefully considered and evaluated every comment and suggestion, treating each person and their ideas with care and respect.

All this was for the sake of one goal: to put together the most helpful book possible on assertive relating. That book is now in your hands. May it bring more assertiveness into all areas of your life.

Kenneth Haugk
Joel Bretscher
Robert Musser

PART 1

What Is Assertiveness?

ASSERTIVENESS SELF-INVENTORY

As you prepare to read this book, it can help to identify the kinds of situations where you find it easier or more challenging to relate assertively. To take a short inventory and evaluate where you currently are in assertiveness, visit **caringassertiveness.org/inventory**.

Relate assertively

A Journey Worth Taking

This book will guide you on a journey worth taking.

Assertiveness brings meaningful, lasting changes in how you relate to people. It helps you communicate your thoughts and feelings more clearly, directly, and honestly while also valuing what others think and feel. It allows you to more effectively voice your own wants and needs, at the same time respecting the wants and needs of others. Assertive relating empowers you to live with greater confidence, care, and authenticity.

When you relate assertively, you'll feel better about yourself, and those you relate to will feel better about you.

Six Important Truths

Despite all the life-changing benefits assertiveness brings, it is often underused or misapplied due to a number of misunderstandings. Here are six important truths that address some of the most common misconceptions and show why you can feel confident deciding to relate more assertively.

PART 1: WHAT IS ASSERTIVENESS?

1. Assertiveness Is Not the Same as Aggression

People sometimes think assertive and aggressive behavior are the same and mistakenly use the terms interchangeably. They might even shy away from anything to do with being assertive because they think it means being pushy, overbearing, and self-centered.

> **Assertiveness** and **AGGRESSION!** are completely different

However, assertiveness and aggression are completely different. Aggression involves relating forcefully to get what you want with little to no regard for others. In contrast, assertiveness involves expressing your wants and needs in a firm yet courteous way that also considers other people's wants and needs. The next chapter will explore the differences in greater detail.

2. You Can Be Direct *and* Kind at the Same Time

People might also assume that being direct is incompatible with being caring and kind, especially when delivering a difficult message. This misconception includes two mistaken assumptions.

- One assumption is that if you want to be caring and kind, you need to sugarcoat your message, hide the truth, and avoid saying anything critical, because being honest and direct would hurt the other person.
- The other is that if you want to be honest and direct with someone, you need to communicate in a tough, hard-hitting manner, because any show of care or kindness would weaken your message.

In reality, it is possible to relate to someone directly *and* kindly, honestly *and* caringly. That's the essence of assertiveness.

3. Respect Is Essential to Assertiveness

People might think of assertiveness as disrespectful. The truth is that assertive relating *is* respectful relating; it involves valuing the other person and yourself. It's not a "my way or the highway" attitude that disregards the other person—or, at the other extreme, a "my needs don't matter" attitude that disregards oneself. Being assertive means relating, acting, and making decisions with respect for all involved.

4. Being Assertive Involves Both Talking *and* Listening

Certainly, a big part of assertive communication involves expressing your thoughts and feelings to another person. However, it also includes listening to the other person as they express their thoughts and feelings to you. Because of the importance of this topic, we've included an entire chapter on assertive listening.

5. Assertiveness Can Be Learned

Whether you're assertive or not isn't written in your DNA. Assertive relating involves a set of skills that can be taught, learned, and enhanced.

> Learning to be assertive is like learning any other set of skills.

Learning to be assertive is like learning any other set of skills—riding a bicycle, cooking, playing the piano, line dancing, or anything else. It may take time and effort to pick up the new skills, but with practice they will become second nature. Even if you've tended to relate passively or aggressively in the past, you can learn a much better approach. If you're already a fairly assertive person, you can continue to strengthen and hone your skills. No matter your level of assertiveness, you will always have room to grow.

6. You Don't Need to Overhaul Your Personality to Be More Assertive

At times people wonder whether becoming more assertive means completely changing their personality. The answer is no—you can practice assertiveness in ways that are authentic and consistent with who you already are and that fit within your cultural context. Of course, in certain situations you will relate differently than you may have in the past, and people who know you may notice that difference. But you'll be the same person you were before—a more confident, genuine, forthright, and respectful version of you.

Growing in Assertiveness Is a Journey

Growing in assertiveness is a journey, and this book will serve as a guide for that journey. Here's a quick look at what lies ahead.

- **Part 1** presents the foundations of assertiveness—what it is and isn't, the benefits of relating assertively, and essential how-to guidelines.
- **Part 2** digs into many situations people regularly encounter where assertiveness is needed, providing principles and suggestions for putting it into action.
- **Part 3** looks at this topic through the lens of Christianity, showing the connections between faith and assertive relating.
- **Part 4** provides additional tools and encouraging words for your continued growth in assertiveness.

The journey toward greater assertiveness is not an instantaneous change; it takes time and intentional effort. It involves recognizing old patterns of behavior and trying out new, more effective ways of relating instead. It will require some refining, stretching, growing, and at times stepping out of your comfort zone. You'll find yourself making deliberate choices every day, looking at your interactions and asking yourself: *What can I do to respond assertively in this situation?*

As you grow in your self-awareness and make these day-to-day choices more regularly, your assertive responses will come more naturally and automatically, and you'll travel farther along the road to greater assertiveness.

Like any other journey, there will be ups and downs along the way, but the personal growth and more meaningful relationships you'll experience will make your efforts highly rewarding. When you make the decision to practice and apply your assertiveness skills, great things will happen.

One final thought: Read this book assertively! Be an active participant throughout. As you read each chapter, try out the suggestions and ideas. See yourself in the examples, thinking about how you have responded in similar situations before—and how you can respond more assertively next time.

The more you immerse yourself in this book, the more it will transform your life and relationships. Let the journey begin!

Passive, Aggressive, and Assertive

Two months after moving into the neighborhood, Jake received a flyer asking for volunteers to help plant some trees in a plot of common ground down the street. Jake was looking for a way to get to know his neighbors, so he signed up right away. Plus, he had plenty of experience. His grandparents had owned a tree nursery in his hometown, and he had worked there several years planting trees.

Jake was one of a dozen people who showed up on Saturday morning. The neighbor heading the project, Matt, divided the volunteers into four groups of three and assigned each group to plant two trees.

As Matt gave the instructions, it quickly became evident to Jake that Matt didn't know much about planting trees. He was telling the groups to dig deep holes, bury the entire root ball, and leave the surrounding dirt sloped inward, which meant a lot of water would flow toward the tree and potentially drown it. Jake knew that the top of the root ball needed to be exposed and the surrounding ground sloped outward to protect the tree.

Here are three ways Jake could respond to this problem.

Option 1: Not wanting to confront Matt and risk making a bad impression, Jake says nothing to Matt or the other volunteers. Instead, he avoids eye contact, nods quietly, and follows Matt's instructions, knowing the trees will probably struggle and die.

Option 2: Jake interrupts Matt and says, "Matt, I don't know what you do for a living, but it sure isn't planting trees. Everything you're telling us to do is wrong, and it'll get these trees killed!"

Option 3: Jake waits until Matt is done talking, steps aside with him out of earshot from the group, and says, "Matt, I appreciate your taking charge of this project—these trees will make the area look really nice. I worked several years at my grandparents' tree nursery, and if we make the holes too deep, the trees are probably going to drown. I'd like to share a few tips I've learned. . . ."

Passive Behavior

In Option 1, by simply going along with Matt's instructions without sharing his own thoughts or ideas, Jake would be behaving in a passive way.

> **Passive behavior** is when a person holds back from expressing their thoughts, feelings, wants, and needs. They are reluctant to make decisions, state their point of view, or take a particular action. Instead, the person goes along with the wishes of others, regardless of what they themselves actually want or what is in their own best interests.

The word *passive* means "not resisting" or "not acting." It was derived from a Latin word meaning "to suffer," which accurately describes what often happens when people behave passively.

> Passive behavior creates an atmosphere of uncertainty.

Passive behavior says "Other people's wants, needs, and feelings are more important than mine," or "I'll give up what I want in order to gain other people's approval or avoid conflict." People who behave passively may hide aspects of themselves to avoid any discomfort, disapproval, confrontation, or criticism. Their opinions can be easily swayed by others, and they may allow others to take advantage of them or make decisions for them.

When people behave passively, they're constantly alert to the potential displeasure and disapproval of others, and they will fine-tune their lives and activities in order to fit in, get others to like them, or gain approval.

Here are some examples of passive behavior.

- When asked to contribute to a decision, the person says, "I don't care—whatever you decide is fine."
- When someone else expresses their opinion, the person automatically agrees, even if they think otherwise.
- In a tense situation, the person slips out of the room to avoid any potential conflict or confrontation.
- In a group setting, the person avoids speaking up, hoping someone else will say what they're thinking.
- The person goes along with what someone else says to do even if they would prefer not to.
- The person apologizes for something that is clearly not their fault.

- If the person doesn't understand something, rather than ask for clarification, they simply nod and say, "Okay."

When someone exhibits passive behavior, it creates an atmosphere of uncertainty where you never really know what they're thinking or feeling. You're left to make assumptions, which can result in hurt feelings, misunderstandings, and strained relationships.

Aggressive Behavior

In Option 2, by ridiculing Matt and his plan, Jake would be responding to Matt with a different form of unhelpful relating: aggression.

> **Aggressive behavior** is when a person relates in a harsh, pushy, or controlling manner. The person puts their own needs, wants, feelings, and opinions above others' and may use demands, insults, sarcasm, manipulation, threats, and other tactics to get their own way.

Often, people relate aggressively to try to get what they want at the expense of others. They communicate "My needs, wants, feelings, and opinions are more important than yours," or even "I have the right to put you down, dominate you, or humiliate you in order to get what I want." Someone who favors aggression has few internal restraints and recognizes few external limits.

Like passive behavior, aggressive behavior often results in suffering—for those on the receiving end and ultimately for the aggressor. If Jake were to relate aggressively, Matt might become defensive, dig in his heels, and ignore any advice, or he might comply outwardly while burning inside. Either way, the confrontation could cast a shadow over the whole group, and the volunteer project would probably struggle to meet its goal. In addition, Jake's aggressive behavior might cause the other volunteers to start distancing themselves from him, hurting Jake's chances to build new relationships with others in the neighborhood.

> Aggressive behavior often results in suffering—for those on the receiving end and ultimately for the aggressor.

Aggression may be nonverbal or verbal, or it may surface as passive aggression.

Nonverbal Aggression

People can exhibit aggression without using words. Common examples include:

- glaring
- a sneer or scornful look
- rolling one's eyes
- an angry grunt, dramatic sigh, or loud "ahem"
- a derisive laugh
- throwing up one's hands
- shaking one's head in disbelief
- pounding a table with one's fist
- pointing at someone in a threatening manner
- standing uncomfortably close
- stomping toward or away from the other person
- slamming a door

Verbal Aggression

Aggression can be exhibited verbally too, taking several forms:

- **Shouting.** Yelling at someone can be a way to intimidate, belittle, or dominate them. Not all shouting is aggressive—sometimes it's necessary in order to be heard in a noisy environment, for instance. However, a loud voice combined with harsh or even demeaning words can feel like an attempt to pressure someone into submission.

- **Insults.** The word *insult* comes from a Latin word meaning "to leap upon." Sometimes people leap upon others with their words, implying that the other person is unworthy of respect.

- **Put-downs.** People use put-downs to call attention to someone's faults or mistakes or to communicate something unflattering about them, building themselves up at the expense of someone else.

- **Blaming.** The word *blame* originates from an old French word meaning "to speak evil of," and that's essentially what someone does when placing blame on another person. Frequently, blame involves insisting on what others should have done based on one's own preferences: "You never should have done that! This is all your fault!" Blaming others is far more likely to escalate tensions than help in any way.

- **Talking over others.** Rather than listening, the person interrupts by speaking louder or more forcefully to take control of the conversation and interject their own thoughts on the matter. It's a behavior that places one's own opinions and desire to be heard above everyone else's.

- **Sarcasm.** The word *sarcasm* in its Greek roots means "flesh tearing"—and sarcasm has the potential to tear psychological flesh. Because it's so commonplace, it may seem like sarcasm shouldn't really hurt, but the condescension and bitterness it often conveys can cause genuine pain, as with Jake's comment, "Matt, I don't know what you do for a living, but it sure isn't planting trees."

Passive-Aggressive Behavior

A subtle form of aggression that can have especially hurtful effects is passive-aggressive behavior.

Passive-aggressive behavior is when a person expresses their anger or dissent in a hidden or indirect manner, with the goal of punishing or controlling others. The person may talk and act in a compliant and agreeable way on the surface while simultaneously taking steps to undermine the decisions or requests of others.

Passive aggression can take several forms, including:

- **Intentional delaying.** The person may say they will do something but then not follow through in order to sabotage other people's goals or plans. Note that delaying is not always a sign of passive aggression; it might stem from perfectionism, disorganization, overextension, or simple forgetfulness. What makes passive aggression different is that the person is capable of doing what was asked but delays purposefully as a means of retaliation or revenge.
- **Pouting.** People who pout are like a teakettle—you know they're heating up because you can see the steam escaping.

Someone who pouts seems to want you to notice they're upset, but they typically won't say why; if you ask them what's wrong, they may quickly and dramatically answer, "Nothing!"

- **Aggravating through details.** The person fixates on certain details to slow down or even stop what needs to get done. Although it's possible for anyone to become fixated on details occasionally, someone exhibiting passive-aggressive behavior does it on purpose to annoy. An example might be when someone is irritated about being asked to set the tables at a community event when they would rather be doing something else. So, they retaliate against the person by spending excessive time scrutinizing, measuring, and adjusting the table settings, making very slow progress in completing the task.

- **Silent treatment.** This behavior involves a person not communicating with someone they're angry at and refusing to respond to them, often without notice or explanation. The motive may be to punish the other person over something they did or said.

- **Bad-mouthing behind someone's back.** The person may quietly comply with someone in the moment but then talk negatively or spread rumors about them as soon as they have an opportunity. They engage in covert means to spread discontent or build opposition to the other person.

In the story, one way Jake might demonstrate passive-aggressive behavior is by making sure his group digs their hole especially deep, with the top of the root ball several inches under the surface and the surrounding ground at a steep slope. He could even tell his group, "That's how Matt wants it," while secretly wanting the tree to die in order to prove Matt wrong.

Assertive Behavior

In Option 3, by taking Matt aside to directly and caringly share his thoughts, Jake takes an assertive approach.

> **Assertive behavior** is a positive, constructive way of relating in which a person clearly, honestly, directly, and confidently expresses their own thoughts, feelings, wants, and needs—while also respecting the thoughts, feelings, wants, and needs of others.

When people relate with assertiveness, they:

- clearly, directly, and kindly express their thoughts and feelings;
- communicate in positive and constructive ways;
- treat themselves and others with dignity and respect;
- act appropriately to make sure their needs are addressed; and
- stand up for themselves and others.

Assertiveness demonstrates a desire and intent to be open, honest, direct, and authentic with others. By behaving assertively, people show that they consider themselves and others to be valued individuals whose feelings, wants, and ideas are worthy of being heard. They express their thoughts directly, honestly, and respectfully, and they affirm others for doing the same. In short, assertiveness says "I respect myself and others—my own wants and needs as well as theirs."

People who practice assertiveness exemplify these attitudes and behaviors:

- **Assertive individuals believe they have choices.** They believe that they are able to exercise self-control and critically examine options and opportunities so they can make the best decisions. *Time*

- **Assertive individuals are proactive rather than reactive.** When appropriate, they enter into situations and propose ideas, offer opinions, or anticipate needs so as to contribute fully instead of simply reacting to people or events.

- **Assertive individuals believe in the value of each person.** They recognize that all human beings have worth, and they are motivated by love to demonstrate care and respect in their relationships.

- **Assertive individuals are people of integrity.** They strive to be consistent in what they believe and how they live. Their external behavior reveals their internal integrity.

- **Assertive individuals accept their own limitations and the limitations of others.** We all have weaknesses and limits to our time, energy, and abilities. Assertive people can live with their own limitations and understand that others also have limitations.

- **Assertive individuals respect their own and others' personal boundaries.** They have a clear sense of self, not allowing others to impose their thoughts, feelings, or wants on them or to control their actions. At the same time, they don't impose on or attempt to control others.

We All Can Grow in Assertiveness

While reading this chapter, you may have recalled times in the past when you related passively or aggressively. If so, keep in mind that nobody is perfectly assertive—at various times everyone exhibits these non-assertive behaviors. We are all works in progress; we all have room to grow.

A good first step in that growth is to identify your past patterns of behavior. By becoming aware of the types of situations in which you've tended to behave passively or aggressively, you'll be able to spot those occasions as they occur and focus on relating assertively instead.

> The more you practice and grow your assertiveness skills, the more natural and instinctive they will become.

As you do, be sure to celebrate your successes and build confidence from them. Also, be kind to yourself when your attempts fall short, looking for ways to learn from those experiences and striving to do better in the future.

The more you practice and grow your assertiveness skills, the more natural and instinctive they will become—and the more consistently you'll relate assertively in all aspects of your life.

Benefits of Assertiveness

As part of our research for this book, we identified people who consistently related with assertiveness and asked them how they would describe someone who acts assertively. Here are the kinds of words they used:

Assertive: straightforward, respectful, trustworthy, honest, authentic, consistent, fair-minded, principled, reasonable, dignified, objective, informed, willing to listen, calm, clear, caring, impartial, inspiring

Compare those to the words they used to describe other behaviors:

Passive: indecisive, weak, frustrating, fearful, evasive

Aggressive: self-centered, demanding, pushy, controlling

Assertiveness is a deeply rewarding behavior that provides many benefits for you and for those you relate to. You will see and experience the richness of these benefits as you grow in this area.

Benefits for Yourself

Here are some personal benefits of building up your assertiveness skills.

Clearer Communication

Assertive communication helps people better receive and understand your message. It keeps your words respectful, your expectations known, and your meaning clear.

In contrast, aggression obscures the message with harsh words and excessive pressure that can lead to confusion, distraction, upset, or anger. Even if it does have the intended effect in the moment, it usually comes at a cost to the relationship. Passive communication, meanwhile, typically leaves the message weak or unclear, unlikely to have the desired impact. Assertiveness avoids both of those pitfalls so you can effectively communicate what you intend.

> Assertive communication helps people better receive and understand your message.

Increased Self-Esteem and Self-Confidence

Assertiveness doesn't simply affect how others perceive you—it affects how you see yourself. As you learn to be more consistently assertive, you will gradually come to see yourself as a calmer, more competent, more confident person. This makes an especially big difference in situations where you may have behaved aggressively or passively in the past, such as when bringing up challenging topics or responding to someone else's strong emotions. Others are likely to see and react positively to your increased confidence and self-esteem.

Healthier Handling of Emotions

Part of assertive relating is being aware of your emotions and handling them in healthy, appropriate ways. Passive and aggressive behaviors get in the way of effectively addressing feelings, leading people to either convey them in unproductive ways or leave them unexpressed. The more you practice assertiveness, the better you'll understand your feelings, and the better you'll know how to recognize, accept, and express them in ways that care for yourself and respect others. You'll feel more comfortable expressing your feelings honestly and freely, and you'll more reliably resist the temptation to overreact by letting your emotions get the best of you.

> Part of assertive relating is being aware of your emotions and handling them in healthy, appropriate ways.

Improved Physical Well-Being

Dealing with emotions in healthy, assertive ways can also benefit your physical well-being. People who most often relate passively or aggressively are more likely to have difficult feelings like anger, sadness, guilt, or isolation build up inside them. These accumulating feelings can increase stress and manifest themselves physically through headaches, heartburn, or sleeplessness. When you practice assertiveness regularly, you can decrease the chances of emotions having a negative physical effect.

Greater Ability to Say No

Too often, when people feel pressured to do something, they say yes when they want to say no. Taking a passive approach,  they surrender their own wants and needs, perhaps due to feelings of guilt or obligation or not wanting to disappoint others. When you live assertively, you free yourself to say no to what you'd rather not do. You can express your no in a firm, kind, respectful way, honoring yourself and the other person.

Greater Ability to Say Yes

Setting personal boundaries by saying no at appropriate times enables you to more freely say yes when you truly want to.  It keeps you from becoming overburdened or overcommitted by taking on so many tasks that you don't have time to engage in activities you truly would enjoy. By practicing assertiveness, when something appealing or important comes up, you'll be better able to respond with an enthusiastic "Yes!"

Improved Ability to Handle Social Pressures

As humans, we often have a strong desire to be liked, paired with a fear of being disliked. That combination can lead us to passively go along with other people's expectations, hoping to win their approval—even when they're pressuring us to do something that isn't in our best interests.

As an assertive individual, you can make your own decisions about what to do and what not to do, regardless of social pressures. You can evaluate what others say on its own merits, without worrying about fitting in or constantly winning others' approval. You're able to simply be true to who you are.

Improved Credibility

Being assertive enhances your credibility in the eyes of others. Because of your straightforward, fair-minded, and principled approach, people will often give greater weight to what you say, more willingly take it to heart, and more consistently put it into action. That doesn't mean they'll agree with everything you say, but they'll usually be more inclined to hear you out and give your words serious consideration because of how you express yourself.

Freedom to Tell the Truth

Assertiveness is about being honest. By living assertively, you enjoy the freedom to speak the truth in a respectful, caring way.

That commitment to honesty doesn't mean you say everything on your mind without considering how those words might hurt others. It does mean, though, that you can talk openly and kindly without feeling the need to bend the truth, sugarcoat reality, or offer false explanations. Such assertive honesty brings a greater sense of freedom to your relating.

Benefits for Those You Relate To

The effects of your assertiveness will touch the people you relate to as well.

Opens the Door for Others to Share Honestly

When you relate assertively, other people feel more comfortable sharing their true thoughts and feelings. Your words and actions build trust, opening the door to more honest, authentic conversations. Not every assertive interaction will lead to deeper communication, but when the situation does call for it, you can lay the groundwork for people to feel safer talking with you.

Helps Others Address Their Emotions More Appropriately

In addition to handling your own emotions, your assertiveness can help others better address their emotions. Your words show that you're comfortable hearing what the other person is feeling, and your calm, collected handling of your feelings establishes a healthy tone for the conversation. As you recognize and manage your own feelings, you'll become more of a calming presence in potentially tense situations where emotions are running high. This encourages others to manage their emotions appropriately and effectively.

Shows Others You Value and Care about Them

Assertive relating makes it clear to others that you see them as fellow human beings who deserve honor and respect. You communicate "I value you. I care about you. I will not belittle, use, abuse, or take advantage of you." Knowing this, other people are likely to feel genuinely appreciated and more at ease around you. If you have an ongoing relationship with them, it can also help take that relationship to a deeper, more authentic level.

> Other people are likely to feel genuinely appreciated and more at ease around you.

Encourages Others to Respond Assertively

Although you can't control someone else's actions, your behavior toward others can affect how they behave in response.

AGGRESSIVE BEHAVIOR INVITES AGGRESSION

Aggressive behavior can cause others to respond aggressively in return. Soon, both people can end up arguing, threatening each other, or putting each other down.

AGGRESSIVE BEHAVIOR INVITES PASSIVITY

At other times, people can become passive in the face of aggressive behavior. When one relates aggressively, the other might quickly give in, apologize for no reason, remain silent, or even walk away.

PASSIVE BEHAVIOR INVITES PASSIVITY

Passive behavior can invite further passivity. When one person remains silent and withdrawn, the other may act the same way. Neither takes the initiative to speak or act, so the interaction goes nowhere.

PASSIVE BEHAVIOR INVITES AGGRESSION

Passivity can also be an invitation for others to act aggressively. When others see someone not standing up for themselves, the passive person may become a target for unreasonable demands, verbal attacks, manipulation, or other such behaviors.

ASSERTIVE BEHAVIOR INVITES ASSERTIVENESS

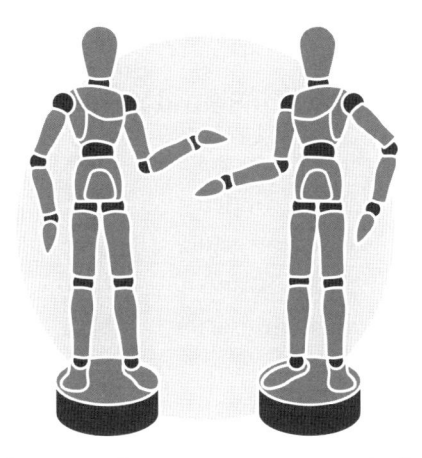

In contrast, when you relate to someone assertively, you greatly increase the likelihood that the person will relate assertively back to you. As you clearly and confidently express your own thoughts and feelings, you encourage others to respond in kind.

In short, relating assertively typically brings out the best in people and makes an assertive response more likely.

Benefits for Everyone

In addition to these benefits for you and the other person separately, each of you benefits together from assertiveness in a number of ways.

Better Conversations

Assertiveness results in better, more meaningful conversations for everyone. It shows your willingness to listen and engage the other person, encouraging mutual respect, honesty, and openness. No one has to spend time guessing what others are thinking, jockeying for an opportunity to speak, or fending off perceived attacks or slights. Instead, the conversation flows naturally and productively.

Better-Defined Personal Boundaries

Assertive relating respects each person's individuality, identity, and autonomy. When you practice assertiveness, you recognize, respect, and maintain boundaries in two important ways:

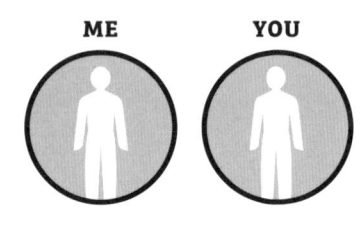

- You protect your own boundaries by not allowing others to impose their will on you and by maintaining responsibility for your decisions and actions.
- You help preserve other people's boundaries by respecting their individuality and not attempting to impose yourself on them or control their decisions and actions.

Acknowledging and safeguarding those important interpersonal lines—and helping others to do the same—is an essential part of healthy, respectful, and responsible relating.

Better Problem Solving

When it comes to practical problems, work projects, relational issues, or any other type of challenge, people are much more effective problem solvers when they approach the situation without feeling threatened and becoming defensive. Assertiveness skills help you activate your clear-thinking, problem-solving self so you can listen well, express both thoughts and feelings, consider options, and work with others to find good solutions.

Even the best solutions may require review and revision, and when you're consistently assertive, you can participate in that process without undue anxiety. You stay focused on finding what will work best for everyone involved, rather than feeling defensive about any changes others propose to your initial solution. In the process, you encourage others to participate in the same way as you solve the problem together.

In contrast to passive and aggressive approaches, which fail to address the central issue and usually make the situation worse, an assertive approach takes a close look at the actual problem and seeks to understand it to develop a solution. Being assertive keeps your attention on the problem and its solutions so everyone can feel good about how you handle difficult situations together.

Stronger, More Authentic Relationships

When you relate to people honestly, clearly, and respectfully, you strengthen your bond with them—in contrast to aggressive or passive relating, which can harm the relationship. In a relationship based on assertiveness, each person feels comfortable sharing their true thoughts and feelings with the other. You can more easily get to know each other without having to worry about manipulative games, half-truths, insincere smiles, or attempts to control others. Even in instances of conflict or disagreement, as you work through those differences while showing high regard for each other, your relationship can become stronger.

> In a relationship based on assertiveness, each person feels comfortable sharing their true thoughts and feelings with the other.

Of course, you will have many assertive conversations without the need to build a close relationship. For the people who are a significant part of your life, though, assertiveness works wonders to make those connections closer.

Easier Living

When people relate assertively with one another, life becomes a lot easier and less stressful. You can count on each other to speak directly, honestly, and with respect, without having to guess what someone really means. There will still be disagreements and conflicts, but you'll be better able to talk through them calmly, listening to one another, and working together to resolve the issue.

Assertiveness enhances living and relating across the board—both for you and for those around you. Although you won't experience all these benefits overnight, you'll see them happen more and more as you consistently relate in an assertive manner. The enhanced communication, significant personal growth, and enriched relationships make it one of the most important relational skills anyone can develop.

4

What to *Say* When You Want to Be Assertive

"It'll be a great time!" Maya said in her voicemail to Nicole. "They've got rock climbing, laser tag, batting cages, retro arcade games, all the stuff Sean loves, and everyone will be there. I can't wait to see the look on his face!"

Nicole found herself in a tough spot. Her brother, Sean, would be turning 30 next week—and Maya, Sean's girlfriend of several months, had just left an excited message about the surprise birthday party she was planning for him. Maya had made a reservation at an entertainment center and secretly invited many of Sean's friends. Because she was going to be busy setting things up, she wanted Nicole to drive Sean there under the pretense of going to a low-key birthday dinner at a restaurant across the street.

But Nicole knew something Maya didn't: Sean hated surprise parties. Nicole had thrown one for him several years before, and it had caught him off guard. She remembered how awkward and uncomfortable he looked the whole time and how, after the party ended, he told her, "I know you meant well, but please don't ever throw another surprise party for me again."

Feeling caught in the middle of a difficult situation, Nicole needed to decide what to do.

- A passive approach would be to say nothing and just let events unfold as they may.
- An aggressive approach would be to tell Maya, "That's a terrible idea! Don't you know that Sean doesn't like surprise parties?"

Nicole decided to take an assertive approach. She cared about both her brother and Maya and wanted to avert a potential problem between them. She knew she needed to be honest with Maya and let her know about the situation. At the same time, Nicole wanted to explain this in a kind and sensitive way because she knew how much time and effort Maya had already invested in planning the party. So, Nicole needed to frame her message both directly *and* caringly.

When you're faced with the need to address a situation assertively, one of the first challenges is figuring out what to say. Here are some suggestions for choosing the right words and expressing them most effectively.

Identify the Real Issue

Before saying anything, identify the core issue that you want to address. Look at the situation as objectively as you can to recognize exactly what you want to communicate. What is the main point, problem, or concern? Knowing that will help you decide what to say.

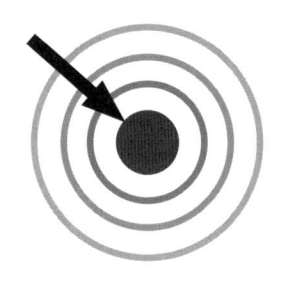

In the story that opened the chapter, the issue for Nicole was clear: Maya wanted to surprise Sean, who doesn't like surprises.

Addressing the real issue would involve letting Maya know about that fact. That kind of response would demonstrate care for Sean, for Maya, and for their relationship.

Speak Up as Soon as It's Appropriate

Most of the time, it's best to immediately address a situation assertively. There are times, though, when it is better to wait. For instance, if emotions are running high, it may be better to delay an assertive conversation until cooler heads prevail. Or, if it's a sensitive issue and you're in a public place, it may be better to hold off until you can talk with the person in private.

It's important, however, not to delay unnecessarily. People will sometimes procrastinate for days, weeks, or even longer, waiting until they have the perfect words or conditions—or hoping the problem will go away. The longer you wait to bring something up, the more challenging it will be to address, and the more likely the problem will intensify. Rather than putting it off, it's far more effective to take the initiative and speak up at the first appropriate opportunity.

If You're Unsure, Ask

At times, people will act in ways that leave us uncertain about their reasons. For instance:

- A coworker hasn't responded to your email.
- Your college roommate doesn't RSVP for your wedding.
- Your spouse hasn't commented on your new haircut.

In situations like these, it's easy to jump to conclusions and assume the worst about another person's intentions, even though there might be a simple, innocent explanation. That's why, if you're ever uncertain about someone's words or actions, the best approach is to ask assertively about it.

Suppose a friend hasn't replied to several text messages over the past few days. Rather than brooding about it, you can call them and say, "I texted you a few times this week and haven't heard back, so I just wanted to check in." Such a direct, honest, and respectful response expresses care and concern rather than assuming the worst. It also opens the door for the person to explain what happened.

Assertively asking about any uncertainties is a great way to prevent hurt feelings and misunderstandings—or to talk over any existing issues and reach a resolution.

Be Honest

Being truthful is foundational to being assertive, so openly and honestly say what you need to say to get your point across. If you dance around the truth, offer false reasons, or disguise what you're really thinking, people may become confused and frustrated, misunderstand your intentions, or possibly feel misled.

A dishonest approach in the opening story, for instance, would be for Nicole to outwardly go along with Maya's plan but then warn Sean in advance and encourage him to play along. Doing that would show disrespect for Maya and her efforts to plan the party. It would be much better for Nicole to just lay out the situation directly and unambiguously.

Here's another example. Suppose you and a friend are going out to dinner, and your friend suggests, "Let's try that Italian restaurant that opened last month." Your friend doesn't know that you went to the restaurant two weeks ago and didn't like the food, so you'd rather not go again.

Don't Say: *"Isn't it kind of out of the way?"*

Do Say: *"I went there a couple of weeks ago and didn't like the food. How about we try somewhere else?"*

The Don't Say example sidesteps the real issue—that you had been there before and didn't enjoy the food. It's unlikely your friend would pick up on that, so they might just respond, "Oh, we can be there in 15 minutes."

In contrast, the Do Say response honestly and clearly lays out your thoughts. From there, you and your friend can pick out a place you'd both enjoy.

Use *I* Messages

Use the word *I* to assertively express your thoughts and feelings to others. Beginning with *I* communicates ownership and responsibility for your statement, and its directness makes it well suited to assertiveness.

Use *I* Messages to Communicate Feelings

You can use an *I* message to communicate how you feel.

- "I'm really glad you can visit."
- "I feel overwhelmed by all the tasks I need to cover today."
- "I'm upset that you didn't clear it with me first."

Use *I* Messages to Communicate What You Want

You can also use *I* to let the other person know what you need, expect, want, or don't want to happen.

- "I want you to stop teasing your sister."

- "I'd like you to hold on to any questions you think of along the way—we'll have plenty of time for them after the presentation."

- "I need to get back home and spend time with my dad since he's really sick."

Combine *I* Messages to Communicate Feelings and Wants

At times you'll combine these two types of *I* messages—saying how you feel and what you want.

- "I find it frustrating when you're late for dinner. I'd like you to come when I call so we can all eat together."

- "I'm really happy with the effort you've been putting into your workouts the past couple of weeks. I'd like you to keep it up for the rest of the season. I think it'll really pay off."

- "I'm worried that Sean won't like being surprised, based on what's happened with other parties. I think it'd be better to let him know about the party in advance and tell everyone else it won't be a surprise—the rest of your plans are great."

Consider another situation: Two roommates have invited several friends over for dinner. One is working hard to get everything ready before guests arrive, but the other is watching videos on their phone. What should the first roommate say?

Don't Say: *"If you really cared about our friends, you'd pitch in and help."*

Do Say: *"I'm feeling stressed trying to get everything done before our friends start arriving. I'd appreciate your help getting things ready."*

In the Don't Say example, the speaker makes it about *you* instead of *I*, fails to express their feelings, and tries to manipulate the other person into helping by implying that it's a matter of whether they really care. The Do Say example makes the request more assertively, with the speaker taking ownership for their feelings and directly saying what they want.

Be Clear and Concise

When you assertively communicate with others, it's best to keep it brief—you don't need to lecture or offer long-winded explanations. People respect and respond to messages that are clear and to the point. Using a lot of unnecessary words can come across as an attempt to avoid saying what you really think, which makes it more difficult for the other person to follow or understand. If the other person has questions, you can answer them as they come.

Suppose a friend invites you to do something during the coming weekend, but you already have other plans, so you need to decline.

Don't Say: *"Well, I don't know if I can go or not. You know how it is on the weekends. I guess everybody's busy on weekends, but I think this is going to be one of the worst for me. There are so many things to do around the house, and I've been saying to myself that I have to catch up on everything. Besides that, we've got old friends from Chicago* coming over on Saturday. They used to live next door to us. They really love plants, and so I've got to get a few flowers in the flower boxes, and I'm already late with all the planting, so it's just going to be a huge rush this weekend. So yeah, I wish I could go with you, but I just can't."

Do Say: "Thanks for asking, but I have a packed weekend already. I have a lot of catching up to do, and we have some longtime friends visiting from Chicago on Saturday. But I really would like to get together with you, so let's plan on another time soon."

Communicate Respectfully

Remember that assertiveness is not just a matter of communicating directly—it's also about communicating kindly. Whatever you need to say, say it with courtesy and care. Treat the other person with the dignity they deserve as a fellow human being. Here are two specific behaviors to avoid.

> Treat the other person with the dignity they deserve as a fellow human being.

Avoid Labeling or Name-Calling

Labeling and name-calling prevent you from owning your feelings, and the other person will probably feel attacked and respond defensively. Instead, identify the specific behavior or actions you're reacting to. Using *I* messages and saying what you want can help you avoid labeling. For example, you're working on a major proposal that you and others will be presenting the following week, and one of the members of the team doesn't seem to be doing their part.

Don't Say: *"You're being really lazy. I don't understand why you haven't been keeping up with your part of the project."*

Do Say: *"I'm frustrated that you haven't done your work for the project. I'd like you to finish your part by Friday so we'll have time to put it all together."*

Note that in the Don't Say example, the speaker aggressively labels the other person as lazy, probably causing more hostility than positive change. In the Do Say example, the speaker assertively communicates by objectively describing the behavior, expressing feelings without attacking the other person, and clearly stating what they want to happen next.

Avoid Sarcasm

Sarcasm is aggressive, so avoid it when you want to be assertive. It's been so normalized that it may seem like an acceptable way to get someone's attention or make a point forcefully, but it belittles others' actions, hides your true feelings, and prevents constructive communication. Suppose your roommate gets home late at night, after you've gone to sleep, and forgets to lock the door—which has happened several times lately.

Don't Say: *"Great job leaving the door unlocked last night again! Why not just send out an invitation to anyone who wants to come in and rob the place?"*

Do Say: *"I noticed this morning that the door was unlocked. Please be sure to lock it when you get home at night. I'd feel a lot safer that way."*

Assertively Repeat Your Message

Sometimes you may need to state your message more than once to get it across. Depending on the situation and relationship, this may involve offering occasional assertive reminders over time, or it may mean restating your point within a single conversation.

Imagine you and your spouse are expecting your first child. The two of you know the gender but have decided not to tell anyone until the baby is born. A well-meaning relative wants you to tell them the secret.

Relative: *"Congratulations! Well, is it a boy or girl?"*

You: *"Actually, we've decided to wait until after the birth to tell people."*

Relative: *"Really? You can tell me, at least."*

You: *"We'd rather not tell anybody until the baby is born."*

Relative: *"Come on. I promise I won't tell anyone."*

You: *"I know, but this is something we want to keep just between the two of us."*

Relative: *"Well, okay, if that's what you want."*

Each time you restate your message, be firm but polite. Remaining respectful and resolute in your response strengthens and underscores your point.

Choosing our words carefully is essential in communicating our thoughts, feelings, and expectations directly, honestly, and with respect. If you exercise these principles, you'll help people better understand and respond to what you say.

5

What to *Do* When You Want to Be Assertive

When you want to be assertive, the words you say are crucial, but they're only part of the picture. *How* you say those words is important too.

In the same way that your words can come across as passive, aggressive, or assertive, so can your nonverbal cues, such as eye contact, facial expressions, body language, or tone of voice. When you align your verbal and nonverbal communication, the message you deliver will be much clearer and stronger.

Here are some principles for assertiveness through verbal and nonverbal cues.

Recognize and Manage Your Emotions

Situations that call for assertive responses may stir up strong emotions, especially if you've tended to relate passively or aggressively in the past. The more aware you are of the emotions you're experiencing, the better you can manage them. For example, if you begin to feel anxious, take a deep breath, relax your shoulders, give yourself some encouragement, and focus on what you want to say.

Taking time to identify your feelings can help you keep them in check, making it easier to deliver your message calmly and assertively.

When Possible, Have an In-Person Conversation

Especially when you're dealing with a sensitive matter or a serious issue, try to have an in-person conversation. Talking face to face allows you to reinforce your words through your body language, facial expressions, eye contact, and tone of voice. It gives you the best opportunity to offer immediate clarification, answer questions, address any uncertainties, and provide additional information. The result is a much more effective communication.

It may not always be possible, practical, or timely to meet face to face. When necessary, talking over the phone or by video chat can be an alternative that still allows for assertiveness, and for simpler, everyday issues it may work just as well. But with high stakes or sensitive issues, try to have an in-person conversation.

Keep Your Nonverbal and Verbal Messages Consistent

Because communication involves both verbal and nonverbal aspects, you need to make sure they match each other. If they seem at odds or even contradictory, the listener is likely to believe the nonverbal message more than the verbal one. Effective communication combines an assertive verbal message with an assertive nonverbal message.

Here are several aspects of communication to pay attention to.

Facial Expressions

Honesty applies to your facial expressions as well as your words. When you're seeking to communicate assertively, look the way you feel. If you're happy, look happy. If you're sad, it's okay to look sad. If you're angry, don't smile. Many people smile when they're expressing anger because they hope to soften the effect, want to avoid alienating the other person, or don't know how best to express their anger in a non-aggressive manner. This kind of inconsistency gives a confusing impression of your intent, making it difficult for the other person to understand what you mean. The mismatch might even come across as patronizing or insincere.

> **NONVERBAL CHECKLIST**
> ☑ Facial Expressions
> ☑ Gestures
> ☑ Body Language
> ☑ Personal Space
> ☑ Eye Contact
> ☑ Volume
> ☑ Tone of Voice

Gestures and Body Language

Use gestures consistent with the assertive statements you're making. Pay attention to how you use your hands when speaking, and do so in a way that feels natural and comfortable to you. Avoid aggressive gestures, such as a clenched fist, pointing fingers, or banging on a table. Likewise, don't use passive gestures, such as wringing your hands or fidgeting with your phone or keys.

Watch out for ways your body language might communicate aggression, like putting your hands on your hips, or passivity, like slouching. Whether the person you're addressing is seated or standing, it's best that you do the same if possible. Also, be sure to respect their personal space. Don't stand too close or trap the person against a wall or in a corner, which could seem aggressive or threatening.

Eye Contact

When you're talking to someone, it's usually best to face them directly and maintain comfortable eye contact. Look at the person in a relaxed, attentive manner that feels appropriate to you based on the relationship, cultural setting, and any other factors. Feel free to occasionally break eye contact for a few moments—locking eyes with someone can feel awkward and possibly give a negative impression. Also, try to avoid looking past the person, constantly shifting your focus, or glancing at your watch or phone, which can convey distraction, evasiveness, or uncertainty.

> With genuine, appropriate eye contact, you'll demonstrate your interest and attentiveness to what others have to say.

With genuine, appropriate eye contact, you'll demonstrate your interest and attentiveness to what others have to say.

Volume and Tone of Voice

Deliver your assertive words with a firm, expressive voice. Speak loudly enough to be heard, increasing your volume slightly as needed for emphasis. Naturally, your tone will vary depending on the content of what you're saying. For example, expressing gratitude calls for a warmer and brighter tone than expressing anger.

Overall, maintaining calm, confident, respectful delivery will enhance the meaning of your message.

Check for Understanding

At appropriate times in the conversation, check that the other person has clearly understood what you've said. For example, you might stop to ask:

- "Does this make sense?"
- "Do you have any questions?"
- "What else do you need to know?"

Questions like these delivered in a calm, respectful manner invite the other person to ask for clarification. You might discover early in the conversation that your listener hasn't taken in everything you've said. That gives you the opportunity to adjust how you're communicating.

Be Ready to Listen

Assertiveness involves two-way communication. Once you've shared your message, give the other person an opportunity to respond, and take time to listen to them. Careful listening contributes to effective, assertive communication because it shows respect for the other person, taking into consideration their thoughts, feelings, wants, and needs.

As you deliver your assertive message, the person may ask for more information, offer an explanation, propose an alternative, or in some other way respond to what you just said. Whatever their reaction, even if it's aggressive or passive, pay close attention and reply assertively. You'll find more on this topic in chapter 15, "Assertive Listening."

Assertiveness integrates words and actions to accurately, congruently, and respectfully communicate what you want to express. All the different aspects of your communication, spoken and unspoken, come together to deliver your message in the most powerful way.

PART 2

Assertiveness Skills in Everyday Life

6

Making and Responding to Requests

Requests are a frequent part of life. Whether you're asking someone to do something for you or another person is asking something of you, you'll encounter these situations regularly.

When it comes to requests, it's important to keep two basic rights in mind: one person's right to make the request and the other person's right to respond with a yes or no or to negotiate an alternative. When you exercise these rights assertively, you show respect for the other person while respecting your own needs, preferences, and limitations.

Consider this assertive conversation between two parents of elementary school children:

Lee: *"The person in charge of planning the spring carnival had to step down yesterday due to some family issues. It was totally unexpected, and we're right in the middle of planning. This is our biggest fundraiser of the year, so we need someone to fill that role right away. Would you be willing to step in?"*

Erin: *"Wow, that's difficult. I know how important the carnival is, but this would be a major time commitment. I need more details and some time to think about it."*

Lee: *"Thanks for considering it. You did a great job planning the Halloween party, so you're the first person I thought of."*

Erin: *"Thanks, I appreciate that. Working on that party was fun, and I know the kids had a lot of fun too. Before I decide on this, could you pull together the information you have—what we've done in previous carnivals, the plans we have so far for this year, and when the leadership team meets? That way I'll know what I'd be getting into. If you can get that to me in the next day or two, I should be able to make a decision quickly."*

Lee: *"That sounds good. I can bring that to you tomorrow. Once you've had a chance to look at it, let's get together to talk. Would that work?"*

Erin: *"Sounds like a plan!"*

Several aspects of this example stand out:

1. Lee gave Erin a clear explanation of the situation and what he would like her to do.
2. Erin expressed sensitivity to the difficulty Lee faced.
3. Both individuals shared feelings and *I* messages, and each listened to what the other had to say.
4. Lee communicated the urgency of his request without begging or pressuring Erin to comply.
5. Erin recognized the urgency but didn't make a hasty decision.

6. Both individuals agreed on when the decision would be made.

7. Both individuals made specific requests.

This kind of assertive approach brings the most positive outcomes.

Requests are a common situation where you'll use the assertiveness principles you read about in chapters 4 and 5. This chapter builds on those principles.

Making Requests

Making even a simple request can be challenging. It may feel risky to state our wants and needs to another person when we don't know how they'll respond. That's where the principles of assertive communication can help.

Clearly State Your Request

This ties in with one of the key principles in chapter 4: When making a request, be clear and straightforward in stating what you want. If there's a specific timeframe involved, be sure to communicate that too.

Don't Say: *"Remember that I told you my daughter is on a swim team? Well, she's doing great lately. She swims mostly backstroke and freestyle, and she does a couple of relays too. Anyway, she has a swim meet coming up next week against their archrivals. It should be a really good one. So, a while ago you said we could trade shifts sometimes if there's a schedule conflict, right? The thing is, I just saw that I'm scheduled to do the evening shift a week from Thursday, which is the same day as my daughter's big meet that I just* mentioned. I'd really hate to miss it. So, I was wondering if you might be willing and able to trade shifts with me—you could cover that one, and I could do one of yours. I mean, only if it's not too big a bother...."

Do Say: "I just saw that I'm scheduled to do the evening shift a week from Thursday, and my daughter has an important swim meet then. Would you be able to take that shift for me? I can take one of yours."

Ask without Unnecessary Delay

As soon as you recognize the need and know you'll want to make a request, ask at the first appropriate opportunity. The person you're asking will appreciate you giving them extra lead time. Plus, the earlier notice makes it more likely that they'll be able to respond positively.

> The person you're asking will appreciate you giving them extra lead time.

Sometimes people are hesitant or uncomfortable about making a request, so they put it off until the last minute. Unfortunately, that generally makes the situation more difficult, inconvenient, and frustrating for everyone.

Avoid Being Overly Apologetic

You have a right to make a request, so there's no need to be overly apologetic for exercising that right. In certain situations, prefacing your request with a brief apology might be the polite thing to do, but avoid overstating it—doing so weakens your request.

Don't Say: *"I'm really sorry to bother you, since I know you're really busy. But if it isn't too much trouble—and I apologize for even asking—could you possibly tell me the name of that cardio test again, whatever you called it, and maybe spell it out? I'm just no good when it comes to medical terms, not the way you are, so if you wouldn't mind spelling it out for me, I'll be sure to write it down so I don't have to ask you again. I'm sorry if this is annoying."*

Do Say: *"I'm sorry to bother you, but could you repeat the name of that cardio test and spell it out so I can write it down? I'd really appreciate it."*

Give the Other Person the Freedom to Say No

Ask in a way that doesn't pressure the person to comply. Don't beg, manipulate, demand, coerce, or make assumptions about their compliance. Make sure the person has the freedom to comfortably say no if they want to decline. For example, suppose you'll be hosting your mother's 80th birthday party, and your friend has an antique farm-themed centerpiece you'd like to borrow since your mother grew up on a farm.

> Make sure the person has the freedom to comfortably say no if they want to decline.

Don't Say: *"That dining room centerpiece of yours would look perfect for my mom's 80th birthday celebration. She grew up on a farm, so I know she'd just love it, and I'm sure you wouldn't want to disappoint her. So, how about I stop by tomorrow afternoon to pick it up?"*

Do Say: *"I'm hosting my mom's 80th birthday celebration, and I was wondering if I could borrow your dining room centerpiece. I think she'd love it since she grew up on a farm."*

Remain Assertive If You Need to Repeat Your Request

With most requests, it may be fine for someone to respond with either yes or no, but there may be certain situations where you fully expect the person to fulfill your request. For example, perhaps you have asked a child to finish packing for a trip, and they haven't yet done so, or you're requesting a refund for a product under warranty, but you're getting the runaround.

> If you need to repeat your request, remain assertive throughout the interaction.

If you need to repeat your request, remain assertive throughout the interaction. You can simply say what you said before, as many times as needed. Don't passively give up on your request right away, and don't slip into aggressive behavior and start yelling, calling the person names, or making sarcastic or condescending remarks.

Saying Yes to Requests

Sometimes people underestimate the power of an assertive yes to a request. When you assertively say yes, you're not just passively going along with it—you're giving the other person your genuine commitment. You're signaling your willingness to get involved, telling the other person you're glad to agree and give your full support.

Saying Yes with Enthusiasm

You may grant some requests unreservedly and enthusiastically. Express your enthusiasm openly and honestly—use *I* messages, and consider what will best communicate your appreciation or excitement to the other person.

Request: *"My fiancé and I have been looking at possible dates for our wedding, and we're thinking August 4th would work best. I know that's eight months away, but would I be able to take off work the first two weeks of August?"*

Passive Response: *"That's fine."*

Assertive Response: *"Absolutely! And congratulations—you must be excited to have set the date!"*

Enthusiastically saying yes to this request is an occasion [opportunity] to affirm the other person's value and your relationship with them.

Your yes can also give you the opportunity to express enthusiasm for a project or cause. Although a simple yes is sufficient, at times you may want to add a supportive *I* message.

Request: *"We're ready to start converting the storage room into a food pantry. Would you be willing to come by Saturday morning at 8:00 and give us a hand?"*

Passive Response: *"I suppose."*

Assertive Response: *"Sure, I'd be happy to help! I really appreciate all the work you all have put into this project, and I'm excited to be part of it!"*

Saying Yes with Conditions

Sometimes you may have reservations about granting a request, but they aren't strong enough for you to say no or negotiate. You can honestly and assertively say yes while also clearly expressing your conditions for fulfilling it. Suppose a friend asks to borrow your lawnmower, but the last time they did so they returned it with a nearly empty gas tank.

Request: *"I need to cut our lawn, but my mower's being repaired. Could I borrow yours?"*

Assertive Response: *"Sure, as long as you refill the gas tank when you're done."*

Saying No to Requests

For many people, saying no to requests is difficult. They may fear that the other person will become angry, feel hurt, or otherwise react negatively. Because of this, sometimes people say yes to requests when they really want to say no.

> Sometimes people say yes to requests when they really want to say no.

But when people agree to do something they really don't want to do, they're not honoring their own rights as a person. They may do the activity begrudgingly, silently regretting their passive yes and even feeling used or manipulated. As a result, they may begin to feel defensive, suspicious, and resentful when others make requests, possibly weakening these relationships.

In reality, saying no is simply an act of recognizing the boundaries between you and the other person. You can certainly decline to do something with or for someone while still valuing them. There's no need to second-guess your decision if the person reacts negatively.

In addition, when people have trouble saying no, they may also have trouble saying yes when they genuinely want to because they're overwhelmed by activities they'd really rather not be doing.

For all these reasons, it's important to become comfortable with assertively saying no to requests. Here are some thoughts about how.

Say No Simply and Politely

A simple, straightforward response is the best way to decline a request. Avoid drawn-out explanations, long sentences, convoluted reasoning, or trying to soften the no with excessive qualifiers and explanations. Also, stay away from the other extreme of being too blunt or forceful with your refusal. Instead, simply, politely, and directly express your no.

> **Request:** "Hey, some of us are going to the baseball game tomorrow night. Want to come?"
>
> **Don't Say:** "Gosh, I really wish I could go, but I've just got so much work to do. I've got a huge report to finish this week, and the kids have soccer games and cheerleading practice. I've got to take them, and that report is going to eat up the rest of my time. I just don't see how I can go. . . . I hope that's okay with you guys."

Do Say: *"Thanks for inviting me, but I can't. This is really a busy week, and I have a lot of work to catch up on. I hope I can go with you next time."*

You Are Not Obligated to Give a Reason

Offering an explanation for declining the person's request is your choice, not an obligation. You can be assertive in choosing whether to give a reason for your no.

You might choose to not offer an explanation when your reason is something private that you would feel uncomfortable sharing, when you don't know the person making the request, or when you suspect the person might try to argue against your reason. In instances like these, a polite but firm no is enough.

When saying no to someone you have an ongoing relationship with, such as a family member, friend, or coworker, it's typically good to offer an explanation to help maintain your positive connection with them.

Repeat Your No Firmly and Kindly If Necessary

As mentioned in chapter 4, you can assertively repeat your message if you need to. If someone presses you to change your mind after you've already said no, repeat your response firmly and kindly—resist the temptation to relent just to stop their insistence. Keep your response brief and simple, without a lot of added explanation. Assertively repeating your no demonstrates care and respect for yourself and the other person.

Be Gracious and Accepting When Others Say No to You

The other side of assertively saying no to a request is assertively accepting a no from someone else. When someone turns down a request from you, accept their no without taking it as a rejection, getting angry, or trying to change their mind. Respond with the same grace and acceptance you would want them to offer you. Doing so shows respect for the other person and keeps the interaction positive.

Negotiating Requests

In some circumstances, it's not possible to give a clear yes or no at first, and you or the other person may need to negotiate the request. This involves getting clarification on issues and assertively proposing changes to help you both decide what to do.

Negotiation is all about dialogue. It means entering a discussion, listening carefully to each other, and trying to reach a mutually acceptable outcome.

For example, perhaps you and a sibling have been planning Thanksgiving dinner for your extended family. You get a phone call the weekend before:

Sibling: *"I just counted up everyone who's coming, and it looks like my house is too small for them. Could we have dinner at your house instead, since you've got more space?"*

You: *"Actually, I'm not sure. It's kind of last minute, and I don't know if I'd be able to get everything ready."*

Sibling: *"I can help out with all that. I could get there early to help with cleaning and setting up."*

You: *"Oh, cleaning isn't a problem; I can take care of that. I'm more worried about the cooking."*

Sibling: *"No worries. I can cook the main dishes and bring them over, and the rest of the family will be bringing the sides and desserts."*

You: *"Okay, in that case it'll work. Just let me know what I need to get ready."*

Respectful, assertive negotiation allows both parties to discuss their needs and work out how they can cooperate to get those needs met. It communicates mutual respect, care, and appreciation even as you express your own limitations.

Here are some guidelines for negotiating a request.

Know That It's Okay to Negotiate a Request

People sometimes respond by reluctantly granting or refusing a request because they aren't certain whether it's appropriate to negotiate. But if you can't give a definitive yes or no, the most assertive response is to suggest an alternative. Even if the person making the request isn't open to negotiating, there's nothing wrong with exploring other options.

> If you can't give a definitive yes or no, the most assertive response is to suggest an alternative.

Don't Use Negotiation to Avoid Giving an Answer

If you need some time to consider or negotiate a request, you have the right to postpone a final decision. Just don't use postponement to put off saying yes or no. Avoiding a straightforward answer is inconsistent with assertiveness. Take the time to get the information you need and think it through to make a good decision, but without delaying excessively.

Making and Responding to Requests

Make Your Goal a Win-Win Outcome

The goal of an assertive negotiation is to come up with a compromise that both parties feel good about. You want to respect your own needs and wants along with the other person's, as opposed to:

- aggressively trying to get as much as possible at the expense of the other person; or
- passively giving in to the other person at your own expense.

For example, a friend asks you to go on a trip together. The last time you did, you had a lot of fun, but you ate at a lot of expensive restaurants, which put a strain on your budget. In this scenario, reaching a win-win outcome might involve negotiating a plan that allows for an enjoyable trip while fitting both of your budgets.

During the course of a negotiation, there may be times when you and the other person realize that a mutually agreeable outcome isn't going to happen. It's okay to end negotiations at that point and decline the request in a kind, respectful way, recognizing the potential disappointment involved.

When you're making or responding to a request, assertive behaviors will serve you well. They will help you move toward the best possible outcome for both you and the person making the request, while increasing the likelihood that the other person will feel respected and cared for.

7

Giving and Receiving Feedback

In our research, many people told us giving and receiving feedback was one of the most difficult areas for being assertive. Here's a sampling of what they said:

"I have one friend who will ask me for feedback, and if I say something critical, she'll get mad or upset. I have another friend who really wants to know the truth. I learned very quickly who to be honest with and who not to."

"When my supervisor asks to see me, I feel the same fear and anxiety I'd have when I was called into the principal's office growing up. I know my supervisor has helpful things to say, but it's hard to shake those fears."

"I asked my brother-in-law to look over my résumé, and when he began to point out problems in it, I started to argue back. He stopped and said, 'If you want, I can just say your

résumé looks great. Or, I can offer suggestions for how to improve it. Which would you prefer?'"

People are often uncomfortable with feedback. Just the thought of needing to give or receive it can stir up anxiety. But even though feedback may sometimes feel a bit unsettling, it is an invaluable tool for helping people grow, giving them an opportunity to improve their work and themselves.

One person we interviewed said that when she was first promoted to a management role, she hired someone to draft grant proposals for her. The drafts were solid overall but consistently had a few problems; rather than give the staff person feedback, though, she would just correct the problems herself. One day, the staff person came to her and said, "Please show me what I'm doing wrong on those proposals and let me correct them instead of you fixing them for me. I want to learn, and if I do, it'll save us both a lot of time and headaches." So, the manager coached her on how to write better proposals. This ended up saving the manager a lot of time, helping the staff person grow, and improving the proposals. Because she provided helpful feedback, everyone benefited.

> Feedback is an invaluable tool for helping people grow, giving them an opportunity to improve their work and themselves.

At different times in life, each of us will find ourselves on both sides of feedback—giving and receiving it. Whether the suggestions themselves are negative or positive, the net effect is a positive one when they're given and received in an assertive manner.

Giving Feedback

Whether it's at work, at home, or elsewhere, we all have opportunities to give feedback. If we want our suggestions to be maximally helpful, the best way to deliver them is assertively. Offering assertive feedback means being clear and direct with the other person, telling them necessary truths in a respectful, constructive manner. Here are some keys to doing that.

Choose the Right Place and Time

The time and setting matter a great deal for how someone will receive feedback, so carefully consider when and where to deliver your message. Assertiveness generally calls for speaking up promptly, but offering critical comments in a public setting with others around can result in embarrassment and defensiveness, making it harder for someone to take in and benefit from the feedback.

[margin note: Not in public]

Sometimes you might not have a choice; circumstances may dictate that you need to deliver the feedback right there and then. If you have the option, however, you may want to wait until you can communicate in private.

Assess Your Motives

The primary motive for offering feedback needs to be care. This could include care for the recipient, helping the person grow or improve in some way. It could also be care for others, including yourself, who may be affected by the person's actions. Feedback that is given simply to insult the person or to blow off steam is rarely helpful. That's why it's important to assess your motives by asking questions like these before addressing the person.

- Do you want to help the person improve a skill or perform a task better?
- Do you hope for them to change a behavior?
- Do you intend to help them learn and grow?
- Do you need to help them address behavior that is adversely affecting other people?

Examining your motives up front will help make your feedback as focused, helpful, and beneficial as possible while conveying your message in a caring and respectful way.

Anticipate Defensiveness

It's a good idea to be ready for a possible defensive response to your feedback. Receiving critical feedback can be challenging, even when it's accurate and kindly delivered, so people may initially react negatively. By anticipating the possibility of such a response, you'll be better able to remain calm and caringly assertive if it happens.

It may help to think of times in the past when you've been criticized and felt defensive yourself. You can draw on those experiences to better understand the other person's reaction and the most assertive way to respond.

When you're offering feedback assertively, the person's initial defensiveness is more likely to fade as they see your good intentions and the value of what you're saying. Even if it takes the person time to process what you've said, often they will come to appreciate your caring approach and adopt a more accepting response.

Offer Calm, Clear, Concise Feedback

To help someone be as open as possible to your feedback, offer it in a calm, clear, concise way.

Calm Feedback

Giving feedback in a calm, non-anxious manner makes it easier to hear, process, and accept. Keep your delivery as relaxed as possible—your calmness will help the other person remain calm as well. Highly emotional feedback is likely to come across as aggressive and push the person on the receiving end to become defensive. If your emotions are running high, wait a moment to regain your composure before addressing the situation.

Clear Feedback

Clearly describe what specifically you have observed and would like to see addressed. Offering details rather than generalities will help you get the message across fully.

Don't Say: *"You need to be more reliable. I just can't count on you."*

Do Say: *"When you get here late, I'm not able to work on our project. I need you to arrive on time."*

Part of communicating clearly is keeping your feedback as objective as possible. Describe the facts and avoid using extreme language, making exaggerated claims, or labeling the person, all of which would make the message less clear and potentially lead to an argument.

Don't Say: *"Your workbench is a disaster! I needed a pair of pliers yesterday, and it took me forever to find one. Stop being such a slob and clean up that mess!"*

Do Say: *"I needed a pair of pliers yesterday, but with all the tools scattered on top of the workbench, it was hard to find. I'd like you to organize your tools so it'll be easier to find things in the future."*

The Don't Say example obscures the feedback and feels like an attack through its extreme words, exaggerated claims, and name-calling, likely shutting down the conversation. The Do Say example uses clear, objective descriptions that the recipient can more easily accept.

Concise Feedback

It's important for your feedback to be concise. Provide enough detail to communicate the points you need to make without turning it into a lecture. The longer you keep talking, the greater the chance that the person will tune out. By keeping your remarks concise, you'll make them easier to digest and respond to.

Be Willing to Listen

After offering your feedback, listen to the other person's response. They might agree with your assessment, express disagreement, ask for clarification, offer an explanation, or react in some other way. They might also share additional information or help you recognize where you need to say more. Whatever they have to say, try to see the situation from their point of view and connect with what they're thinking or feeling. You don't have to agree with them, but it's important that you listen to understand where they're coming from.

> Feedback is often most helpful and effective when it's collaborative.

The person might not respond immediately because they need to think through what you said. Give them time to reflect on the feedback, and then, if you need to, invite them to respond by saying something like:

- "I'm interested in hearing your thoughts about that."
- "What do you think about making these changes?"
- "How would you feel about giving these suggestions a try?"
- "What ideas do you have about what to do next?"

Feedback is often most helpful and effective when it's collaborative, with both of you contributing thoughts and ideas to find the best way forward.

Stand behind Your Feedback

It's important to stand behind what you say and not backtrack. If the person responds in a highly emotional way, it can be tempting to soften, withdraw, or even apologize for the feedback, but that would undermine the intended message and prevent the person from benefiting from it. Suppose you have just shared some difficult truths with someone, and the person begins to cry.

Don't Say: *"I'm sorry, I shouldn't have said anything."*

Do Say: *"I know this is tough to hear."*

Similarly, if the person reacts defensively, gets angry, or questions your motives, assertively hold to your original message.

Don't Say: *"Never mind. Forget what I said."*

Do Say: *"I'm telling you this because I really care and want to help."*

If it later becomes clear that your feedback was off base, you can correct yourself. However, if the feedback is valid and was expressed in an honest and caring way, there's no need to withdraw it.

As Appropriate, Offer Support

There may be instances in which you offer ongoing support to the person as they implement the changes you suggested. For example, if you're offering feedback to a colleague or someone you supervise, you might check in periodically to provide coaching, encouragement, or assistance. You wouldn't do this in every situation or with everyone, but it can be another way to help the person grow.

Don't Overlook Providing Positive Feedback

When someone only offers critical comments, others may tune the person out or distance themselves. To prevent that, be sure to offer positive feedback as appropriate. This doesn't mean you have to balance every suggestion for improvement with a word of praise, which can seem formulaic or insincere, but do consider how you might genuinely affirm the person. When you offer a good mixture of affirmations and suggestions over time, the person will be much more willing to take what you say to heart. Chapter 10, "Giving and Responding to Compliments and Appreciation," talks more about positive feedback.

> ### A NOTE ABOUT GIVING FEEDBACK IN A WORKPLACE
>
> The assertiveness principles described so far apply to offering feedback in almost any setting, including work settings. Many workplaces have additional policies and procedures for feedback. If you're giving someone feedback in a place of work, by all means relate assertively, but also be sure to follow your workplace's guidelines.

Receiving Feedback

In addition to being assertive when giving feedback, it's also important to remain assertive when we're on the receiving end. Even when the feedback is valid and caringly offered, it may require some intentional effort to refrain from reacting defensively, making excuses, or rejecting the communication outright. So, when someone offers you feedback, keep an open mind and look at it as an opportunity to learn. You might even consider asking for their suggestions for improvement at times.

Here are some guidelines for assertively receiving feedback.

Seek to Hear the Message Fully and Accurately

Listen carefully to be sure you understand what the person is actually saying. If necessary, check with them about how accurately you've understood what they've said. You might say:

- "If I understand right, you're telling me . . . *[state what you have heard]*. Is that what you mean?"
- "Let me check this out. You're saying . . . *[state what you have heard]*. Is that accurate?"

Restating

This kind of response can also let the person know you are indeed interested in their feedback. It invites them to confirm the accuracy of your perceptions or clarify their point.

Be Aware of Your Emotions

When listening to critical remarks, it's not uncommon to experience feelings such as defensiveness, embarrassment, anger, fear, or confusion. Difficult emotions in the face of negative feedback are normal, but they can sometimes interfere with our ability to hear, process, and benefit from what others tell us. That makes it important to pay attention to your feelings so you can better handle them.

> Being open to feedback is the best way to make growth happen.

It can help to remember that making mistakes or needing to improve in some areas doesn't reflect badly on you as a person. Every one of us has room for growth, and being open to feedback is the best way to make growth happen. Recognizing that truth can make it at least a little easier to manage challenging emotions related to feedback.

Pause to Reflect

After the other person has shared their suggestions, take a little time to let the words sink in and think through them. Avoid letting your immediate emotional reaction take over. You might even tell the person you need a few moments to process what they've said and collect your thoughts. Pausing also gives you the opportunity to consider what questions you might have or whether you need additional information.

Keep in mind that people offering feedback typically mean well. Most often, they see an issue that needs to be addressed and genuinely want to help. It usually takes a good amount of courage to speak to someone about a perceived need for change. Pausing instead of offering an immediate, potentially non-assertive response shows respect for their effort and their good intentions.

Assess the Feedback

As you pause, carefully consider the feedback. Assess it as objectively as possible so you can weigh its helpfulness and best use it for your growth.

> Look beyond the message's delivery and assess its meaning, content, and validity.

If the feedback was presented assertively, it will likely be easier to receive, process, and take to heart. The care and respect behind the words can help you move past any initial discomfort or embarrassment to fully consider the suggestions themselves.

When feedback is presented non-assertively, it can be tempting to disregard it immediately without any consideration. However, just because someone's delivery is aggressive or passive doesn't mean that their comments are entirely invalid. There still may be some truth in what they said.

Suppose you accidentally give someone the wrong deadline for submitting an important application. They end up sending their application late, and when it's rejected, they yell at you and call you stupid because of your mistake. Although their reaction is aggressive, it doesn't change the fact that you did make an error and, because of that, need to pay more attention to details in the future.

Look beyond the message's delivery and assess its meaning, content, and validity. You can then draw from it any useful ideas that can help you learn and grow.

Respond Appropriately Based on the Situation

Once you've heard and assessed the person's feedback, respond in an appropriate way, focusing on remaining assertive throughout. The specifics of how you respond will vary, depending on the nature of the feedback and the situation.

> No matter what the situation is, remain assertive in how you respond.

- If the feedback is valid, thank and affirm the person for offering it. You might also ask the person for additional suggestions or guidance if that would be helpful.

- If you're uncertain about anything the person said, ask for clarification.

- If the feedback seems inaccurate or invalid, find out more about what the person is thinking—for instance, "I want to make sure I understand what you're saying. Could you give me some more details?" If further discussion confirms your initial impression, you can thank the person for sharing their thoughts.

- If the feedback points out mistakes or areas where you've fallen short, apologize as appropriate and seek to do better in the future. At the same time, don't beat yourself up over what happened. We're all human, and we all have areas for growth.

No matter what the situation is, remain assertive in how you respond, and affirm the other person for sharing their thoughts.

Feedback is not something to dread; it's an act of care and an opportunity for growth, something to welcome and encourage. Assertiveness helps you and others make the most of feedback and realize greater growth.

Offering, Asking for, and Accepting Help

At various points, all of us may find ourselves in need of help or in a position to offer help. That's a natural part of life—helping and being helped lifts everyone up.

But despite that reality, all too frequently people don't get the help they need. On one side are those who would really benefit from help but don't seek or accept it, possibly because they feel embarrassed about their need or worry about compromising their sense of independence. On the other side are people who are in a position to help but don't offer it. They may feel uncertain about how their offer will be received or have concerns that they'll appear pushy, nosy, or intrusive. Whatever the reason, when help doesn't happen, people tend to struggle much more than they need to.

> Openness to both helping and being helped benefits everyone.

That makes it important for all of us to cultivate the ability to assertively offer help to others—and to assertively ask for and accept help when we need it ourselves.

Offering Help

If you see someone who could use help, and if you're in a position to provide what they need, feel free to assertively make the offer. It's a great, tangible way to support someone experiencing a life challenge, large or small, and show that you care.

People sometimes wonder how they can best offer help in a way the other person will welcome. Here are some suggestions.

Picture Yourself in the Other Person's Situation

A good starting point is to put yourself in the other person's situation. Consider what they're dealing with, what they may be feeling, and what needs they may have.

Doing this can give you a better awareness of the different types of help the person could use, which provides a starting point for how you might extend the offer. Just as importantly, if the person is hesitant to ask for or accept help, your efforts to understand can reassure them of your interest and care.

It may not be possible to fully understand everything going on inside another person, but your empathetic mindset can still help you make a connection with them and be better prepared to meet their needs.

Communicate That You Definitely Want to Help

When you make your offer, make it clear that you truly want to help—communicate your sincerity. This is important because a frequent practice is to say something vague or noncommittal.

OFFERING, ASKING FOR, AND ACCEPTING HELP

Don't Say: *"Let me know if you need anything."*

Do Say: *"I've been thinking about how I could give you a hand. Here are some possibilities, in case any of them work for you."*

Don't Say: *"Text me if there's anything I can do."*

Do Say: *"You've got a lot going on, and I'd really like to help lighten your load. What do you need most right now?"*

The Don't Say statements are less effective for two reasons. First, even if the offer to help is sincere, it can come across as rote and obligatory, leaving the person wondering whether the words are genuine. Second, the offer puts the burden of asking for help on the one who needs it, when they might not have the energy or inclination to reach out right now. As a result, many people don't respond to these non-specific offers and instead continue trying to handle things alone.

The Do Say statements, meanwhile, make it clear that you're ready and willing to help—that you're not just saying what's expected. They show real interest in the other person and openness to their needs.

If the person still seems hesitant, you might repeat your offer to communicate your willingness to help.

You: *"I want to help out. What would you like me to do?"*

Friend: *"I don't want to put you out. I can handle things myself."*

You: *"I know you could do it by yourself, but I'd be happy to help. What can I do?"*

It's important not to pressure the person, but assertively repeating your offer reassures them of your sincerity and makes it more likely they'll accept.

Ask the Person What Type of Help They Might Need

The prior two examples point to another good principle: When you aren't sure exactly what kind of assistance someone could use, go ahead and ask. They're the best expert on their own needs, so they can point you toward the areas where you can make the biggest difference.

Try to avoid asking questions that can be answered with yes or no.

Don't Say: *"Do you need any help?"*

Do Say: *"What can I do right now that would help you the most?"*

The Don't Say example asks whether the person needs help, which is easy to answer with a quick no. The Do Say example gets the person thinking about what types of assistance they could use at that time, making it more likely that they'll agree to receive it.

Be as Specific as You Can

In some situations you might already have a good understanding of the person's needs and ways you might help. In these instances, rather than making a general offer, you could suggest specific ways you might assist and perhaps even when. Here are a couple of examples of how to do that:

- "I'm raking my yard this afternoon, and I know you're dealing with a lot right now. I'd be glad to rake yours too."
- "I have some free time on Wednesday afternoon, so I'm available to do some cleaning or run some errands then. What can I do to help?"

People are much more likely to say yes to offers that address specific needs. Of course, if someone needs something entirely different from what you're offering, be flexible and willing to help in other ways as you're able.

Treat the Person with Dignity and Respect

When people are going through difficult times, one of the biggest barriers to accepting help is not wanting to appear vulnerable or needy. They might feel self-conscious or even ashamed of their situation. If the person offering help gives the impression that they're making a noble gesture to someone less fortunate, the one in need of help is likely to feel belittled or disrespected, and the odds of a negative response go up sharply.

So, when you offer assistance, treat the person with dignity and respect. Relate to them as an equal, and help them feel safe opening up. Communicate with humility, as just one person reaching out to another. Make it clear that you're glad to help, without making a big deal of your actions. When someone can tell you're approaching them as a person, not a project, they'll be more comfortable accepting your offer.

> Make it clear that you're glad to help, without making a big deal of your actions.

Follow Up If the Answer Is No

What if someone turns down your offer to help? It's important to respect their wishes, but depending on the relationship and the circumstances, you might follow up later to see whether their needs have changed. Perhaps the person didn't need help right at that moment, but now they do. They might not have been quite ready to accept help, or they might have wanted it but just weren't sure your offer was genuine.

Whatever the case, it's caring and assertive to check in and offer help again later, perhaps a few days, a couple of weeks, or longer depending on the situation. Without being pushy, gently remind them of your offer.

- "I mentioned earlier that I'd be glad to help you during your treatment—with yardwork, running errands, cooking, cleaning, or anything else. I wanted to check in again and let you know the offer still stands."
- "Last Saturday, I offered to pick up some things for you on my grocery run, and you didn't need anything then. I'm heading to the store again this afternoon, so I thought I'd ask if you need anything this time."

You wouldn't do this in every situation, but if someone you know is dealing with some significant, ongoing needs, it's often a worthwhile step.

Six Reasons to Receive Help

In our research, people said they are much more open to helping someone else than they are to asking for or accepting help themselves. Being the helper gives you a sense that your life is generally stable and that you're secure enough to reach out to someone else. Being in need of help, on the other hand, brings the discomfort of not being self-sufficient and of seeing aspects of your life potentially beyond your control. In light of all that, it can be challenging to admit to such needs.

> Embrace your humanness by receiving help when you need it.

It is worthwhile, though, to recognize and embrace your own needs to receive help. Here are six important reasons:

1. **Receiving help shows care and respect for yourself.** It gives you valuable support during a difficult time and prevents you from neglecting your own needs.

2. **Receiving help benefits the helper.** People experience satisfaction when helping others, so giving someone that opportunity is meaningful for both of you.

3. **Receiving help can avert needless pain.** When you let others help, they can reduce your burden and keep your struggles from worsening. There's no need to try to tough it out on your own—let others support you through it.

4. **Receiving help can benefit your loved ones too.** The challenges you're facing may affect those you're close to. When you hurt, they hurt too, and depending on the circumstances, they may have additional responsibilities connected to it. Your receiving help provides welcome relief for them as well.

5. **Receiving help saves time and energy you can focus elsewhere.** Especially in a more significant crisis, you may find yourself stretched thin trying to handle everything yourself. Allowing others to help meet certain needs can give you greater capacity to focus on other issues.

6. **Receiving help is part of being human.** All of us go through difficult times when we would benefit from the help of others. That doesn't make us weak, just human. Embrace your humanness by receiving help when you need it.

Asking for Help

Whether it's for a minor need or a major crisis, asking for help can make a significant difference in your life—and often, people around you will be willing and eager to help. There's no need to feel reluctant to ask for help when you need it. The following tips can make it easier to ask.

Identify People You Could Ask

Think about who may be available or have the necessary abilities to do what you need to get done. Sometimes this may be a matter of who's nearby, such as if you need help putting your bag in the overhead bin on an airplane, or if you need someone to hold the door open when you're carrying a heavy box. For more significant or ongoing needs, you might think of one or more people you know who are dependable, available, and able to lend a hand.

Determine What Types of Help You Need

At times, your specific need for help may be immediate and obvious. However, especially in a more serious crisis, you might have multiple needs, including some you wouldn't think of at first. That's why it's good to consider what types of help would benefit you the most, possibly putting together a list of areas where you could use a hand.

Everyone's needs are different, but here are some areas where people can often use help during a time of crisis:

- Providing, preparing, or coordinating meals
- Caring for children
- Doing yardwork or household chores
- Providing transportation
- Shopping or running errands
- Picking up mail or packages delivered to the house
- Caring for pets
- Making phone calls
- Offering respite for a primary caregiver by staying with an ill family member for a few hours
- Providing a listening ear

> Thinking about your needs ahead of time makes it easier to quickly and confidently let others know of specific ways they can help.

Thinking about your needs ahead of time makes it easier to quickly and confidently let others know of specific ways they can help.

Clearly Communicate Your Needs

When you're asking for help, clearly and directly communicate your needs to the other person. The more specific you can be about the type of support and when you need it, the better.

- "Tomorrow morning I'm headed out of town for a couple of days, and there's a package coming to my house in the afternoon. Could you check my porch tomorrow evening and pick it up for me?"
- "I was wondering if you'd be willing to watch the kids Thursday morning while I'm at the dentist."

Letting others know exactly how they can help at any given time gives them the best opportunity to support you.

Accepting Help

When others offer help, even if it would meet a genuine need, people sometimes still struggle to accept it. Because of the benefits to both the one needing help and the one offering it, though, it's worth overcoming that reluctance. You don't need to carry the burden alone; you can give yourself an invaluable break by saying yes to someone else's offer to assist you. Here are some suggestions for accepting help.

Say Yes When You Do Need Help

First, when an offer of help comes your way and you genuinely need it, give yourself permission to respond with an assertive yes! Graciously accepting their support shows care and respect for yourself and the one extending the offer.

Sometimes people worry that accepting help leaves them indebted to the other person or requires them to return the favor at some point in the future. That's not the case, though; you might have an opportunity to help them sometime down the road, but you aren't obligated to do so. Most often, a simple thank-you is enough to show your appreciation for their caring act.

If You'd Prefer a Different Type of Help, Say So

Someone may come to you with a genuine offer of help that doesn't line up with what you need. If so, it's perfectly okay to assertively tell the person you don't need that kind of help and to suggest other possibilities instead.

Neighbor: *"Since Rachel is sick and you may not have much time to cook, I thought I might bring over dinner for the two of you tonight."*

You: *"I appreciate the offer, but a few people have brought us meals lately, and our fridge is full. What I could use most is someone to walk our dog every once in a while so I can stay here with Rachel."*

If you've come up with a list of needs, you can draw on that list to give them ideas. You can feel confident about offering these suggestions—people are likely to appreciate knowing what they can do to make the biggest difference for you.

Recognize That It's Okay to Say No

While it's important to say yes to help when you need it, you can feel free to say no assertively when you don't need or want help. You might have to decline because of privacy issues, boundaries, safety concerns, not needing help right then, or other reasons. You can express your appreciation while assertively declining.

- "Thanks for offering, but I don't need help with that right now."
- "I appreciate the thought—for now, though, I'd rather take care of it myself."

Although it's important to receive help when you need it, you are not obligated to accept every offer. Certainly be open to the possibility, but the final decision is up to you.

Openness to both helping and being helped benefits everyone. It gives people the support and assistance they need to handle challenging times, it offers the satisfaction of caring for someone in a practical way, and it builds community and trust in relationships.

> It's a privilege to be in either role—one life touching another during a time of need.

Whether you're the one providing help or the one receiving it, remember this point: You are two human beings in different situations in life. Under different circumstances or at another time, your roles could easily be reversed.

It's a privilege to be in either role—one life touching another during a time of need. Welcome these moments when they come.

9

Expressing and Receiving Anger

Anger is a difficult emotion for many. In our research on situations where people found it most challenging to be assertive, anger was consistently at or near the top of the list.

For many people, the difficulty comes from not knowing how to express their own anger or even whether to express it at all. They worry about losing control if they do let it out. Or, they're concerned about what others will think or how they'll respond. Many struggle with knowing how to react to someone else's anger—whether to shrink away, give in, or argue back. Because of these challenges, anger can become a source of deep anxiety, confusion, apprehension, and guilt.

Anger in itself isn't inherently a problem. It's a powerful feeling, but it's still a feeling like any other. Anger only becomes an issue when people express or receive it aggressively or passively. It's not a problem when handled assertively, as in this example.

Nick is buying a used piano and has arranged to have his brother Kyle help him move it. At 8 A.M. on Saturday, Nick is in front of his house with a rented truck, pads, dolly, and winch straps ready as planned—except Kyle doesn't show up. Nick calls and texts Kyle several times, but since the truck rental is only scheduled for 90 minutes, he finally gives up and asks his next-door neighbor to help instead.

> Anger in itself isn't inherently a problem.

After the move is finally done, Nick is rolling the ramp back into the truck when Kyle pulls into the driveway and says, "Sorry, sorry! I totally forgot to set my alarm. But I see you were able to get the piano moved without me, so it looks like everything worked out okay."

Nick is furious—with good reason. He now has a choice in how he can express that anger to Kyle.

Nick (Aggressive): *"I can't believe you! We had this planned for days, and then you don't even bother to show up until it's done, and you think everything's okay? You're as irresponsible as always. I should have known better!"*

Nick (Assertive): *"Actually, Kyle, I'm pretty angry right now. You said you'd be here to help, and you weren't. I did get the piano moved, but I had to ask my neighbor to help, which I hadn't been planning to do."*

Nick knows from past experience that reacting aggressively will only lead to a heated argument. Another, more passive option would be to try to bury his anger, but he knows that won't work either. So, Nick decides to go with the assertive response.

Now Kyle faces his own decision about how to respond to Nick's anger.

Kyle (Aggressive): *"I already said I was sorry! It's your fault for deciding to do this at 8 on a Saturday morning anyway! Did you ever think that people might want to get a little extra sleep on the weekend?"*

Kyle (Assertive): *"You're right. I agreed to come at 8, and I messed up. There's no excuse for that. I'm sorry."*

Kyle appreciates the assertive way Nick expressed his anger, so he opts for the assertive response.

Now it's Nick's turn. Although he's still upset, Kyle's respectful response has softened his anger a bit. Nick chooses to respond assertively as well.

Nick (Assertive): *"Part of the issue is that I had to ask my neighbor at the last minute. He had to rearrange some of his plans, and I felt bad about that. Plus, because of all that, I won't get the truck back in time, which means I'll have to pay for an extra hour."*

Several times while Nick is talking, Kyle feels tempted to jump in to defend himself, but he doesn't. He knows Nick has a right to be angry, so he listens and waits for Nick to finish before responding.

Kyle (Assertive): *"I didn't think about the truck rental. I'm sorry. I'll pay for the extra hour."*

Nick (Assertive): *"You don't have to do that, but I appreciate the offer."*

Kyle (Assertive): *"I know I let you down, and I'm really sorry about that."*

Nick (Assertive): *"Thank you. I'm still a little upset, but I'll get over it—and I accept your apology."*

Assertiveness in sharing or responding to angry feelings has the potential to strengthen and deepen relationships by allowing both people to talk honestly about difficult issues and work toward a resolution.

While none of us will probably ever be totally comfortable dealing with anger, as you build your assertiveness skills, you will become increasingly confident relating in this challenging area.

Know Your Typical Reactions

Chapter 2 mentioned the value of knowing how you tend to act in certain situations. This is especially true with anger. A good first step in learning to handle anger more assertively is to know how you've typically dealt with it in the past. When you feel angry:

- Do you deny or try to hide the feelings?
- Do you lose your temper, shout at people, and possibly call them names?
- Do you express your anger assertively, letting the other person know honestly and respectfully what you're thinking and feeling?

Similarly, when someone shows anger toward you, how do you tend to respond—passively, aggressively, or assertively? The more aware you are of your own behaviors, the better you'll be able to change those behaviors in the future.

In addition, it's helpful to identify any specific types of situations or conditions that more frequently spark angry feelings inside of you. For example, are there certain topics, issues, individuals, or circumstances where you become defensive, argumentative, or frustrated? Knowing this can help you better recognize and handle any potentially volatile situations in the future.

> The more aware you are of your own behaviors, the better you'll be able to change those behaviors in the future.

Expressing Anger

People sometimes think that anger is always aggressive, but that isn't necessarily true. Anger can be expressed assertively, which is beneficial in several ways.

- It clearly and courteously communicates your feelings and the reasons for them to the other person, which minimizes the potential for misunderstanding.
- It gets your strong feelings out into the open, relieving any tension inside.
- It encourages the other person to respond in a similar, assertive way, giving the best chance for a genuine conversation and a positive resolution.

Here are some guidelines for assertively expressing anger.

Take Ownership of Your Anger

Before you can do anything with your anger, you need to acknowledge, accept, and take ownership of it. Another person can't "make" you angry. Their words and actions can certainly affect you, but your emotional response is ultimately based on your own perception of the situation. Recognizing that the anger you feel is your own, not someone else's, gives you a stronger starting point for dealing with it.

When you're angry to any degree, great or small, it's important to acknowledge it. By taking ownership of your feelings and committing to expressing them in healthy, assertive ways, you enable yourself to address your anger proactively instead of reactively.

Pause before Speaking

When you feel anger growing, before saying or doing anything, pause for a moment. Stepping on the brakes gives you an opportunity to collect your thoughts and avoid saying or doing something you may later regret.

For instance, if you tend to express anger aggressively, that momentary pause allows you to calm yourself at least a little so you can stay patient and respectful. Or, if you often handle anger passively, you can use the time to bolster your courage.

It's also helpful to assess the actual focus of your anger. If you don't intend it to be directed at the person you're speaking to, make that clear to them.

Assess What You Know and What You Don't Know

It's helpful to think through the circumstances as objectively as possible, determining what you do and don't know about the situation. Ask yourself: What do you know for a fact? What uncertainties remain? Are you making assumptions to fill in any gaps?

For example, suppose you arrive home from work to find a messy kitchen—flour on the countertops, splotches of batter on the floor, and dirty mixing bowls and cake pans in the sink. It seems clear that your children are the culprits, and you feel anger rising up. Before yelling at them, however, you stop and think—and realize that, based on the evidence, they're probably planning to surprise you with a cake for your birthday tomorrow.

Being clear about the knowns and unknowns will help you manage your response and avoid jumping to conclusions or making faulty accusations.

Communicate Calmly

After you've paused and prepared yourself, communicate your message as calmly as you can. All the points from chapter 4 apply—in particular, "Identify the Real Issue," "Use *I* Messages," and "Be Clear and Concise."

Start by communicating how you feel and, as appropriate, why you feel that way. Remember to own your anger and don't accuse the other person of making you angry.

> **Don't Say:** *"You knew what I told you was a secret, and you blabbed it to everyone anyway! You humiliated me in front of all my friends, you jerk! I'll never trust you again!"*
>
> **Do Say:** *"I'm angry because what I told you was private and personal, and you shared it with others after I asked you to keep it a secret. I'm really embarrassed that others know about it now."*

The Don't Say statement is disparaging and accusatory and will likely put the other person on the defensive. The Do Say example, meanwhile, owns the anger, clearly states the reason for it, and maintains dignity and respect.

Depending on the circumstances, you may communicate what you want the person to do. Suppose a colleague tells you he just promised a client that your team would complete a project in two weeks, even though a realistic timeframe for a project of that size would be a month or more.

Don't Say: *"You said what?! You're crazy—there's no way we can do that! How in the world could you make such a ridiculous promise to a client?! Anyone with half a brain would know we'd need at least a month! Don't ever go off and make a stupid promise like that without talking to me!"*

Do Say: *"Honestly, I'm upset you made a promise like that. Two weeks isn't enough time to finish this kind of project. I'm going to need your help explaining this to the client and figuring out where to go from here. Next time, check with me first before making that kind of large promise to a client."*

The Don't Say example lets the anger out in an aggressive way. The Do Say example expresses it much more calmly and then clearly states what you want to see happen.

Stay in the Here and Now

When expressing your anger, focus on the immediate issue that prompted your anger and avoid dragging past mistakes, negative personal history, or earlier problems into the discussion. Bringing up past difficulties can weaken the specificity of your message, leaving the person confused over what you're actually angry about. It also risks shifting the message into accusations that "you always" or "you never" do something, which increases the possibility that the person will stop listening and become defensive.

For example, suppose at a family gathering your brother makes a sarcastic comment about your son being clumsy and unathletic. This upsets you greatly—primarily because it feels like an attack on your son, but also because your brother made many similar remarks about you while growing up.

Don't Say: *"Cut that out! You insult people all the time, and it's not funny. You did that again and again to me when we were growing up. I hated it then, and I hate it even more now that you're saying it about my son! Now knock it off!"*

Do Say: *"That remark was very upsetting, and it could have been devastating for my son if he'd heard it. Please don't make comments like that about him."*

The Don't Say example strays outside the here and now, focusing mainly on the sibling's past behavior. The Do Say example keeps the focus on the current issue and handles the problem assertively.

If any past issues or repeated behaviors do need to be addressed, find another time to discuss them rather than when you're angry over a specific incident.

Maintain Respect

Assertiveness involves respecting both the person you're relating to and yourself, so no matter how intense your feelings may be, treat the other person with respect. Doing so keeps the lines of communication open and makes it more likely that your message will have the intended effect. On the other hand, labeling the person, name-calling, making sarcastic remarks, or otherwise putting them down will probably inflame the situation or shut down communication.

This applies to respecting yourself too—don't let anger at yourself turn into self-directed attacks. For instance, if your hand slips while you're taking a pan of lasagna out of the oven and it falls and spatters all over the kitchen floor, don't call yourself names or beat yourself up over it. It's fine to feel and express anger, but go easy on yourself.

Give the Person a Chance to Respond— and Then Listen

After you've expressed your anger, give the other person a chance to respond. They may reply in many different ways— an apology, an explanation, a defensive argument, a correction or clarification, or possibly little to no response. Whatever they may say, listen with an open mind and respect the person even if you disagree with what they have to say.

> Hearing the other person's response helps you gain a more accurate picture of the situation and possibly clear up misunderstandings.

Hearing the other person's response helps you gain a more accurate picture of the situation and possibly clear up misunderstandings. It fosters the kind of two-way communication necessary for true assertiveness.

Receiving and Responding to Anger

The difficulties with anger aren't just in expressing it; being on the receiving end can be challenging too. When confronted by another person's anger, sometimes people retreat rather than face it head on; other times they respond by getting angry themselves, possibly escalating the situation. If responding to anger is a struggle for you, you're not alone.

Thankfully, practicing assertiveness provides you with a much more effective way to handle someone else's anger when it is directed toward you. Here are key points for doing so.

> **IMPORTANT NOTE**
>
> These principles apply to most situations in which another person is expressing anger to you, but an important exception is when there's a threat of violence, including situations that may involve abuse. If you find yourself in a situation where another person's anger may turn violent, take any appropriate steps to avert danger and ensure your own safety and the safety of others.

Hear the Person Out

When someone expresses their anger toward you, hear them out; listen without cutting them off. This is important for three main reasons:

1) Interrupting the person to interject your own thoughts typically only intensifies their anger.

2) After you've listened, you can more effectively respond to the person, and they'll be much more likely to hear what you have to say.

3) When you've allowed the person to fully voice their anger, often they'll calm down and be better able to talk things through.

Of course, while letting the person vent, show respect for yourself as well by setting good boundaries. If, as you hear them out, they cross the line and their words become demeaning, you might say, "I'm willing to hear what you have to say, but not if you're going to talk to me like that. I'd appreciate it if you would just tell me what's going on."

Be firm but calm, composed, and respectful in your response. If necessary, bring the conversation to an end, but do so without losing your temper. Aggressively ending the conversation can worsen negative feelings, which can be especially damaging if you have an ongoing relationship with someone. An aggressive example could be yelling, "I'm done with this conversation!" and then storming off.

Remain in Touch with Your Own Emotions

When dealing with someone's anger, pay attention to the emotions that may rise up inside you: defensiveness, indignation, fear, distress, guilt, or anything else. The greater your awareness of your own feelings, the better you can keep them under control and maintain a calm, non-anxious demeanor. The calmness you exhibit can have the same effect on the other person.

Avoid Knee-Jerk Reactions

As the person expresses their anger, they might say something that touches a nerve or ignites an emotional reaction, giving you the urge to interrupt. You might feel the sudden need to offer a defense or denial, saying something like "That's not true" or "You're all wrong!" Or, you might be tempted to say, "Don't be angry," or "Calm down" in an attempt to put a stop to their anger.

These and other knee-jerk reactions will likely only increase

> Resist the impulse to interrupt; instead, focus on listening to the person.

the person's ire and make the exchange even more heated. Resist the impulse to interrupt; instead, focus on listening to the person. Maintaining your composure as you allow the other person to communicate fully is typically the quickest and most effective way to help the person work through their emotions.

Identify the Message behind the Person's Anger

Intense anger can affect how clearly a person communicates. They may say things they really don't mean, especially if they are relating aggressively. It may take extra effort, but do your best to understand the message the person is actually trying to communicate beyond their angry words. Think through questions like these:

- "What exactly is the person angry about?"
- "Who is the person actually angry at?"
- "How much responsibility, if any, do I bear?"
- "What does the person expect from me?"
- "What other emotions might the person be experiencing below the surface, potentially affecting their anger?"

In some instances, you might discover that you aren't even the focal point of the person's anger. They may actually be angry at someone or something else but simply venting their feelings at you. In these situations, by patiently listening to the person as they get their anger out, you are providing them with a great opportunity for relief.

Make Understanding Your Goal

When anger enters the picture, it's easy for tempers to flare on both sides, arguments to intensify, and divisions to widen as each side focuses on winning. The best way to prevent this is to concentrate on understanding the other person so you can better see where they're coming from.

> Let go of your biases and judgments, at least for the moment, and try to see the situation from the other person's perspective.

Let go of your biases and judgments, at least for the moment, and try to see the situation from the other person's perspective. You don't have to abandon your own point of view and give in to them—just try to understand them better.

When the person senses that you really are listening and making a genuine effort to understand, often their anger will subside and they'll be more open to doing the same. There's no guarantee that they'll reciprocate or that you'll come to an agreement, but your understanding does a lot to reduce the tension and bring both parties toward greater acceptance.

Empathize

Empathizing means stepping into the other person's perspective, connecting with their feelings, and then acknowledging and validating what they're going through. A simple response such as "No wonder you're mad" or "That really must have hurt" can have a powerful soothing effect—communicating that you've heard what the person said, connected with their feelings, and care about what they're going through. Even if you disagree with the root cause of someone's anger, you can still empathize with them by recognizing and acknowledging the hurt, pain, frustration, or other emotions they may be experiencing.

> Even if you disagree with the root cause of someone's anger, you can still empathize with them.

Empathizing with someone who is angry has several important effects.

- It lets the person know that you really are listening, which they may not experience all that often. You're taking the time and making the effort to learn about and understand what they're dealing with.

- It shows the person that you care about their feelings and what they are going through—that they really do matter to you.

- It validates the person's feelings as real and important. People too frequently *invalidate* a person's anger by saying, "Don't be angry," or "You shouldn't feel that way." Statements like these suggest that the feelings are somehow wrong, which nearly always leads to a more intense reaction.

All this can work wonders to defuse the situation and resolve angry feelings.[1]

---

[1] For more on this topic, see *The Gift of Empathy: Helping Others Feel Valued, Cared for, and Understood* by Joel P. Bretscher and Kenneth C. Haugk (St. Louis: Stephen Ministries, 2023).

PART 2: ASSERTIVENESS SKILLS IN EVERYDAY LIFE

Respond Appropriately

After listening and gaining an understanding, give an assertive response based on what's most appropriate to the situation. For instance:

- You might offer a sincere apology or make amends if the situation calls for it.
- You might say yes or no or negotiate an alternative if the person made a request.
- You might ask for clarification or offer an explanation and then listen some more.

However you respond to the person, speak calmly and clearly, honestly and directly.

Through your assertive handling of anger, you will model a more effective way of relating. When you *express* anger assertively, you communicate difficult feelings and realities in an honest, respectful way that reduces anxiety, builds trust, and paves the way for solutions. And, when you *receive* anger assertively, you help calm others' emotions and demonstrate your understanding and care. Because anger is a challenge for so many people, your ability to handle it assertively will be a gift to everyone around you.

> Your ability to handle anger assertively will be a gift to everyone around you.

10

Giving and Responding to Compliments and Appreciation

Mark Twain once wrote, "I can live on a good compliment two weeks." Often, people are slow to express their appreciation, so we may need to live on a good compliment for more than two weeks. That's why this topic is so important. Sharing a few heartfelt words with someone at the right time can give them a wonderful lift.

The Benefits of Compliments and Appreciation

Giving compliments, praise, and encouragement is just as beneficial a part of the assertive lifestyle as any other. People typically enjoy being appreciated; it boosts confidence and self-esteem, cultivates healthy relationships, and fosters meaningful growth. It's also easier for people to accept well-intended, helpful criticism if you've shared genuine affirmation with them in the past.

Praise may affirm what people already know or hope to be true about themselves, or it may point them toward new self-understanding. Although many people have some idea of what they do well and the talents and skills they possess, that picture may not be complete. A compliment can help people learn more about themselves and their unique strengths—such as when you tell someone, "You're really good with kids," or "You're an excellent listener," or "You do a great job making complicated ideas easy to understand," when they'd never thought of themselves that way before.

> Compliments and appreciation are part of the feedback people rely on to assess themselves and grow.

Compliments and appreciation are part of the feedback people rely on to assess themselves and grow. People tend to repeat behavior that is appreciated and avoid or reduce behavior that is ignored or met with disapproval. Receiving praise is important for identifying positive behaviors and, in turn, encouraging a person's growth.

Reasons People May Not Share Compliments or Appreciation

Despite the importance of this relational tool, many people hesitate to offer compliments. Sometimes they assume that compliments aren't necessary because someone already knows their strengths. Other times they think that the person already experiences fulfillment doing those things and doesn't need any praise for it, or that the person has received plenty of compliments already. They might also consider it unnecessary because the person is simply doing what is expected of them. Because of all this, they conclude that their positive words won't have any real impact.

Personal discomfort can also be a factor. People can feel self-conscious, embarrassed, or emotionally vulnerable offering words of appreciation. They may worry how the person will respond or interpret what they say. Whatever the reasons, when people neglect to offer praise, they prevent others from receiving the benefits of their affirming words.

Giving Compliments and Appreciation

Overcoming barriers to offering compliments and appreciation is very worthwhile. Following are a number of ideas for how.

Seize the Opportunity

First of all, embrace opportunities to offer someone a compliment or word of praise. So, if you're thinking about telling a customer service person how much you appreciated their help, go for it. If you enjoyed a soloist's music, let them know. If the crème brûlée someone prepared was delicious, tell them that. Allow yourself to say what's on your heart in an authentic, spontaneous expression of appreciation.

> Sharing a few heartfelt words with someone at the right time can give them a wonderful lift.

Don't Worry about Finding the Perfect Words

One reason people may hesitate to offer praise is concern about coming up with exactly the right words. They worry that if they don't express their thoughts perfectly, the other person will take it the wrong way, so they decide against saying anything.

But the precise words you choose don't matter as much as the sentiment behind them. If you express your praise sincerely and supportively, your meaning will come across. The person hearing your appreciation will remember the overall meaning and the resulting feelings more than the words you used.

Make Your Compliment Specific

Whenever possible, focus your compliment or appreciative statement on a specific behavior. Clearly state what you like and why. A specific compliment is more likely to be believed and appreciated than a general comment.

For example, your friends have just moved into a new home, and you're visiting them for the first time. They've spent a great deal of time and energy decorating, and you can tell that they're justifiably proud of their work.

Don't Say: *"Everything looks nice."*

Do Say: *"I like the paint—it's really bright and cheerful. You put a lot of thought into picking out the new furniture too. It all fits together so well!"*

Avoid Putting Yourself Down

Sometimes people feel the need to pair a compliment for someone with a criticism of themselves. By drawing a comparison, they hope to make the praise seem even more special. In fact, the criticism adds an uncomfortable note that shifts the focus away from the one being complimented and may make the person feel obligated to affirm you in return.

Don't Say: *"I love how neat your office is! I wish I could make mine look that good."*

Don't Say: *"Your painting is beautiful! You're so talented—I can barely draw a stick figure."*

Don't Say: *"These cookies are so good. I can't bake to save my life."*

In instances like these, stop after the compliment and avoid adding a put-down about yourself. By keeping the focus fully on the other person, you keep your compliment assertive and meaningful.

When Necessary, Affirm Your Original Statement

If someone struggles to assertively receive your compliment or praise, follow up with a brief affirmation of your original statement. You don't need to belabor the point, but make sure your appreciation comes across. Suppose you want to compliment a colleague after a presentation.

You: *"That was an excellent presentation, especially how you explained what brought us to this point."*

Colleague (Passive): *"Oh, it's just part of my job."*

You: *"That may be true, but I really appreciate the quality and thoroughness of what you do, and I wanted you to know that."*

Simply reasserting your compliment helps emphasize your genuine feelings.

Be on the Lookout

Many opportunities to offer a compliment are easy to spot, so take advantage of those moments and offer people the appreciation they deserve. It's also good to stay intentionally on the lookout for other opportunities. All too often, people's praiseworthy actions go unacknowledged, or they hear more about what they've done wrong than what they've done right. Taking a moment to recognize what they've done and express your appreciation not only validates their actions but affirms them as a person.

So, keep your eyes open for situations that call for affirmation, and then offer it. These unexpected compliments can go a long way toward brightening someone's day.

Receiving Compliments and Appreciation

Offering a compliment can take courage. When you graciously and assertively receive a compliment, you demonstrate respect for the person who gave it and their courage in speaking up.

People often brush off compliments or struggle to accept praise. Sometimes this is because they don't believe they deserve it. Other times they may question the motives of the person who offered the kind words. Or, they might mistakenly think that accepting a compliment makes them seem less humble. But dodging, downplaying, or ignoring compliments can give the impression that the person's words aren't really appreciated, which can discourage them from offering compliments in the future. Plus, it causes someone to miss out on the full experience of receiving affirmation.

Here are some thoughts about receiving compliments and appreciation assertively.

A Simple "Thank You" Will Do

When someone offers you a compliment or praise, it's perfectly fine to respond with a simple "Thank you." Trust the person's good intentions and enjoy their kind words.

Don't Feel Obligated to Offer Praise in Return

After receiving a compliment, you don't have to give one in return or search for something to praise about the other person. You certainly can if you want to, but it shouldn't be out of a sense of obligation; people can tell if you're only returning the compliment because you think you have to. Your sincere thanks will show your appreciation.

Avoid Invalidating the Compliment

Few would deliberately insult someone who offers them a compliment, but people often do so inadvertently. For example, a friend says, "Your garden is so beautiful!"

Don't Say: *"It's nothing special."*

Do Say: *"Thanks. I'm glad you like it."*

The Don't Say response invalidates the compliment and even indirectly implies that the one giving the compliment doesn't know what they're talking about. In contrast, the Do Say response affirms the other person by thanking them and communicating "The fact that you like my garden is important to me."

Make Your Nonverbal Message Match Your Verbal Message

Your nonverbal messages can either add to or detract from the way you receive compliments and praise, so make sure they're consistent with each other. That may include behaviors like maintaining eye contact, offering a smile or warm expression, and showing confident body language.

For instance, a coworker has been ill and missed work for two weeks. During that time, you've covered many of your coworker's tasks. On his first day back in the office, he stops by your desk and lets you know how much he appreciated your help.

Don't: Stay turned away from your coworker, look at the floor, fidget, and mumble, *"I was happy to do it, and I'm glad it was helpful."*

Do: Give your coworker your full attention, make good eye contact, smile, and say clearly, *"I was happy to do it, and I'm glad it was helpful."*

There's No Expiration Date for Compliments

There is no time limit for offering a compliment, gratitude, or appreciation to someone who has done something special for you. Even if the event happened years ago, your comment about it today can touch someone's life.

A woman shared with us a story that illustrated this. When she was in high school, she was anxious and uncertain about her path in life. She felt drawn to art but lacked confidence in her abilities and career prospects. Her art teacher took great interest in her work, offered a lot of affirmation and feedback, challenged her to grow, and overall helped her find the right path. She ended up pursuing a graphic design career and was happy and successful in the field.

Decades later, she happened to think of how her art teacher had helped get her started on that path, and she wanted to express her gratitude. So, she wrote her teacher a letter saying how much that encouragement and guidance so long ago meant to her. The teacher got in touch not long after, saying, "It means a lot to hear about the difference I made in your life. Thank you."

Whether it's in the moment or even decades after the fact, if you have an opportunity to share your appreciation with someone, go for it! It will be a blessing for both of you.

> Whether it's in the moment or even decades after the fact, if you have an opportunity to share your appreciation with someone, go for it!

11

Assertively Choosing to Act Passively or Aggressively

In most situations in life, relating assertively is the best approach. Every once in a while, however, circumstances arise in which a passive or aggressive response might be more appropriate or perhaps even necessary. In such instances, you can make an assertive decision to act in a passive or aggressive manner.

Keep in mind that this kind of occurrence is rare and not how you're likely to relate the vast majority of the time. When such instances do arise, though, you can carefully consider the circumstances and make a deliberate choice to respond to the situation in a passive or aggressive way.

Assertively Choosing Passive Behavior

Occasionally, behaving in a passive manner can show care for another person, strengthen a relationship, or help preserve safety. Again, it's an exception rather than the rule, and it's not a course of action to choose simply because remaining passive seems easier than relating assertively. Instead, it's a matter of a passive response being the best, most appropriate course of action in a specific time and place. That may happen in situations like these.

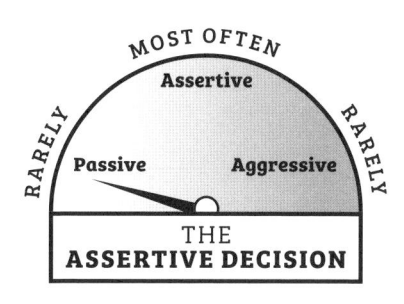

When Someone Is Already Apologizing

When a person is already apologizing for something they did, you may choose not to respond assertively so as to avoid coming across as needlessly critical. If the person has taken responsibility and expressed their regret, there's usually no need to point out the mistake. You might not even bring up the hurt or inconvenience resulting from the person's actions.

Suppose you find out that a friend recently invited several others out to lunch but didn't ask you. You feel hurt and left out, but before you can ask about it, your friend comes to you and apologizes profusely, saying they inadvertently left you off the group invite.

Even if you still feel disappointed over not being included, you might decide to let it go and say, "No worries—let's do lunch together sometime soon."

When Assertiveness Might Add to the Person's Pain

It's possible that, due to the timing or extenuating circumstances, assertiveness at a particular moment might add to someone's pain, such as when they're dealing with a personal crisis. In these instances, it's better to hold off on what you want to say until that person is better able to listen and respond.

For example, you might be planning to have a candid talk with your teen about a recent incident of irresponsible behavior, but that day they come home in tears, saying they lost the student council election. The most caring response is to postpone your planned conversation and focus right now on your child's disappointment.

When It Really Isn't a Big Deal

You might sometimes choose to respond passively when the situation isn't a big deal. You could decide to address it assertively, but there's no pressing need to, and you and those around you aren't seriously affected.

Picture yourself waiting in line to enter a concert hall. As you approach the entrance, a couple of people jump in line right ahead of you to join a group of friends. You might feel annoyed, but because the delay is minimal and your seats are reserved, you decide you can easily ignore it.

> When something truly isn't a significant issue for you, you can assertively choose not to react.

Be careful about how you decide what isn't a big deal. Sometimes people define it very broadly and become passive and appeasing when they shouldn't be, allowing others to walk all over them in situations that genuinely call for an assertive response. A situation may also seem minor at first but then persist and worsen over time. When something truly isn't a significant issue for you, though, you can assertively choose not to react.

When Assertive Behavior Might Put You in Danger

If behaving assertively might put you at risk of harm, passive behavior may be necessary. For instance, if you are being robbed, insisting on your rights could increase the chances of serious injury or worse. Assertively choosing passive behavior in this kind of situation is typically a safer course of action.

Similarly, if you encounter someone who is angry and seems at risk of becoming violent, you'll likely want to avoid any kind of confrontation. It's best to behave passively until you're out of harm's way.

Assertively Choosing Aggressive Behavior

Although rare, there are situations where the best course of action is to respond in an aggressive way. Note that this is not the same as actually being aggressive. You aren't reacting in an impulsive, uncontrolled, contentious manner—rather, you are making an intentional, proactive decision in a specific situation to take necessary and appropriate actions that appear aggressive.

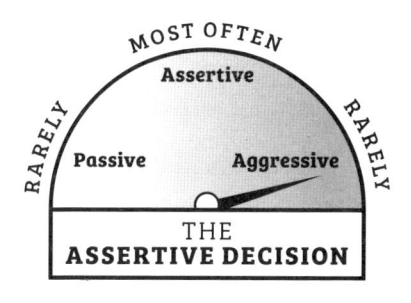

These instances should be few and far between, and only when there's no other viable option. The most important key is to maintain control—to recognize the need for an aggressive action, make a deliberate choice to respond in that manner, avoid going too far, and return to assertive behavior as soon as possible. Because aggressive actions carry great potential for causing harm or escalating tensions, it's vital to take a moment and assess the conditions before deciding what to do.

Here are a few questions to consider first. If the answer to any of them is no, then it's best *not* to respond aggressively.

- **Is the aggressive action a proportionate response to the situation?** Aggressive behavior should be avoided unless it's a serious, high-stakes situation where people's well-being depends on it.

- **Is the aggressive action the only way to achieve the needed result?** Such behavior is a last resort, to be used only in those rare instances where assertiveness isn't an option.

- **Will you be able to maintain control of your feelings and behavior if you take an aggressive action?** The moment one loses control, an aggressive act is no longer an assertive choice.

If you decide to go forward with it, once you've taken the necessary action, return to assertiveness as soon as possible. Avoid staying in an aggressive mode any longer than you need to.

Here are three examples of situations that might call for assertively choosing to relate aggressively.

To Protect Someone from Imminent Danger

When people are in immediate danger, you may need to act aggressively for their safety. Suppose you're in a building that's on fire, emergency responders have not yet arrived, people are panicking, and you know the evacuation route. You may need to shout out commands to get everyone out of

In emergency situations, taking an aggressive approach may be the most caring way to proceed.

the building quickly and safely. In emergency situations with no time to spare, taking an aggressive approach may be the most caring way to proceed.

To Get People's Attention

Usually, you'll be able to get people's attention through assertive behavior. On occasion, however, possibly because the environment is loud and raucous or because others are ignoring your assertive attempts to settle a crowd, you might need to take an aggressive action. These are instances when someone might slam a book down, pound a gavel, or let out a loud, shrill whistle—actions that in normal circumstances might seem aggressive but at the time are needed to regain control.

An oboe player in a regional orchestra shared with us how their conductor grew frustrated during one rehearsal because other musicians were talking loudly while he was trying to work with one section. Despite being asked multiple times, the musicians wouldn't quiet down. Eventually, the conductor threw his baton down, stepped off the podium, and glared at them silently with his arms crossed. The orchestra members immediately quieted down, and the rehearsal resumed.

To Make a Clear, Unmistakable Point

In addition, there may be times when your assertive attempts to communicate haven't worked and an aggressive action is necessary to make a point quickly, clearly, and unmistakably. Although this kind of action may catch people off guard with its aggression, it's an assertive choice when you do it in a determined, controlled way—especially when the action runs completely counter to your typical behavior.

One man in our research described a vivid memory from childhood. During a family Thanksgiving dinner, some of his aunts and uncles began arguing about an incident from many years in the past. The discussion kept getting louder and more heated and threatened to ruin the gathering.

Finally, his grandfather, who was typically calm and soft-spoken, pounded his fist on the table, stood up sharply, and shouted, "Quiet!" Everyone immediately went silent, taken aback by the radical shift in the man's usually dignified demeanor. The grandfather continued, "We are a family. This is Thanksgiving. If you want to argue, take it outside—don't do it here!" After a long silence, the grandfather sat down and calmly said, "Now, let's enjoy our meal." Their dinner proceeded peacefully after that.

Note that these momentary acts of aggression can lose their effectiveness when overused, so it's best to stick with assertiveness whenever possible. On occasions where you need to communicate bluntly and unmistakably, however, it can be effective to briefly shift away from your assertive standard.

Depending on the situation, assertively choosing passive or aggressive behavior may be the best course for you. In deciding to use one or the other, allow care and respect for yourself and others to guide you.

PART 3

A Faith Perspective on Assertiveness

A NOTE ABOUT PART 3

Thus far, this book has taken a how-to look at assertiveness. We've explored what it is, what makes it important, and how to put it into action in daily life and in specific types of situations.

The next three chapters take a different approach—they look at assertiveness from a Christian faith perspective. You'll see how Jesus and the Bible provide an excellent model for living assertively and how assertiveness is consistent with the Christian lifestyle.

People who read this book may come from different religious backgrounds or none at all. Whatever your beliefs, we invite and encourage you to read these chapters. They can build on what you've read so far and add a new dimension to this topic.

12

Jesus as a Model of Assertiveness

When it comes to describing the character of Jesus, many different words may come to mind—*gentle, humble, patient, compassionate, loving, forgiving, self-sacrificing,* to name just a few. The word *assertive,* on the other hand, probably isn't the first one people think of.

But a closer look at Jesus' life reveals that he was a model of assertiveness. He spoke, taught, and acted with clarity, directness, and kindness. He expressed his emotions appropriately without being controlled by them. He recognized and acknowledged the value and worth of each person, whether they supported or opposed him. Everything he did, he did with firm intention and conviction, carrying out his mission and doing what he knew was right while resisting social pressure. He never lost sight of who he was and what he came to do.

> Everything Jesus did, he did with firm intention and conviction.

This chapter shows how Jesus modeled what it is to live assertively, pointing out key examples from his life.

PART 3: A FAITH PERSPECTIVE ON ASSERTIVENESS

Seven Ways Jesus Was Assertive

While his circumstances differed from our own, Jesus' words and actions provide us with principles we can apply throughout our lives.

1. Jesus Was Assertively Compassionate

Wherever he went, Jesus was surrounded by people who needed help. Time after time, he assertively chose to address those needs out of love and compassion, offering physical and spiritual healing. Jesus saw the value of each individual and sought to care for the whole person.

- Mark 2:3–12 tells about a few individuals who wanted Jesus to help their friend afflicted by paralysis. Because the room where Jesus was teaching was packed with people, they lowered their friend down on his mat through an opening they had made in the roof. Seeing the man's need for both physical and spiritual healing, Jesus first spoke to the man's spiritual condition, which critics in the crowd didn't think he had the authority to do. Undeterred, Jesus courageously chose to show his compassion and send a message about his authority. He then healed the man physically by saying, "I tell you, get up, take your mat and go home."

  > We too can make the choice to treat others with kindness, care, and respect.

- In Luke 8:41–48, Jesus was walking with an influential synagogue leader who had urgently requested him to come to his house to heal his sick child. While they were walking through the crowd, a woman who had been an outcast for over a decade because of a chronic illness, desperate for healing, touched the edge of Jesus' cloak and was made well. Immediately, Jesus stopped and asked who had touched his cloak. When the woman timidly approached and told him what had happened, Jesus proclaimed, "Your faith has healed you." Even in the midst of many others desiring his attention, Jesus made an assertive, compassionate choice to acknowledge this woman, and by doing so, he gave her the dignity she had missed for years and the restoration she had longed for.

Jesus assertively chose to be compassionate, seeing each person as worthy of respect and intentionally putting them and their needs before himself. We too can make the choice to treat others with kindness, care, and respect, no matter who they are.

2. Jesus Assertively Resisted Pressure from Others

Throughout his ministry, Jesus faced frequent pressure from others to act in certain ways. But he remained committed to his mission, holding true to who he was and what he had set out to do. His integrity was a hallmark of his life.

> Jesus knew who he was and allowed his clear understanding of his mission to motivate everything he said and did.

- Luke 5:27–32 describes a time when Jesus invited Levi, a tax collector, to become one of his disciples. Doing so upset the social expectations of the day; people widely viewed tax collectors with disdain since they worked for and profited from the occupying Roman government. Levi held a banquet for Jesus, where they ate together with other tax collectors and many others who had been ostracized from society. When religious leaders confronted Jesus about keeping such company, he assertively responded, "It is not the healthy who need a doctor, but the sick." Because he was confident in who he was and deeply committed to his mission, he resisted the pressure to stay away from those whom society had deemed unworthy.

- In Mark 10:13–16, Jesus was teaching when many parents started bringing their children to him for his blessing. Jesus' closest disciples tried to stop them, believing their busy teacher didn't have the time for that. But Jesus became indignant and said to them, "Let the little children come to me, and do not hinder them, for the kingdom of God belongs to such as these." He spoke up and didn't waver from his purpose, even when his disciples tried to impose their own views about how to carry out his ministry.

Jesus knew who he was and allowed his clear understanding of his mission to motivate everything he said and did, whatever opposition he faced.

3. Jesus Assertively Handled Requests

As Jesus' fame spread, more and more people came to him with requests, and he brought requests to others as well. We can learn much from the assertive way Jesus handled these situations.

Jesus consistently and assertively said yes to requests that would improve the lives of others and were aligned with his ministry.

- One such situation was illustrated in Mark 9:14–29 when a father asked Jesus to heal his son, who had uncontrollable fits of self-harm and seizures. The father was desperate but skeptical about what Jesus could actually do. Jesus didn't let any of that bother him and calmly agreed to heal the

JESUS AS A MODEL OF ASSERTIVENESS

boy. He made a deliberate choice to take action despite the father's uncertainty.

Jesus also assertively refused requests when he knew they weren't made with others' best interests in mind. He wouldn't allow requests like these to get in the way of his ministry.

- Throughout Jesus' ministry, he spoke about the kingdom of God, based on loving one another and sharing God's goodness. Jesus' disciples, though, assumed that this kingdom would be established through force, with Jesus overthrowing the dominant political powers of the era. In Mark 10:35–45, two of these disciples, James and John, requested to have the two most powerful places of authority in this new earthly kingdom. This upset the other disciples because they wanted the most power for themselves. Jesus knew this desire for power was motivated by self-interest. He refused the request and then told the entire group that true greatness comes from serving others. He used the misguided request as an opportunity to gently but firmly help the disciples change their perspective.

> Jesus told the entire group that true greatness comes from serving others.

Jesus was confident enough to ask assertively for what he needed, <u>not holding back out of a fear of rejection or inconveniencing others.</u>

- As described in Matthew 4:18–22, Jesus asked his twelve closest disciples to follow him throughout his ministry, knowing they would be giving up a lot to do so. For the disciples Peter, Andrew, James, and John, that meant giving up their trade as fishermen. Even though these requests were significant, Jesus clearly and confidently gave the invitation without any coercion when he said, "Come, follow me." In so doing, he demonstrated the power of assertiveness in making major requests.

Jesus also didn't let social barriers keep him from making requests.

- In John 4:7–42, Jesus and his disciples were traveling through Samaria. A Samaritan woman came to draw water from a well where Jesus was sitting, and Jesus asked her for a drink. This was unthinkable at the time due to deep-seated animosity between the Jewish and Samaritan people, not to mention the expectation that men didn't make requests of women in public. Jesus' request surprised the woman, but it provided an opportunity for a life-giving conversation that enriched the woman spiritually and led her to reexamine her life. She was so moved that she ran into her village to tell others about the conversation, which intrigued them and convinced them to meet Jesus themselves. Jesus' initial, assertive request met his immediate need for water but also had a much wider impact on many people's lives.

> Jesus handled requests with confidence and directness, in all things guided by his love for others.

Whether Jesus was responding to or making requests, he did so with courageous assertiveness. He handled them with confidence and directness, in all things guided by his love for others.

4. Jesus Assertively Responded to Anger

Jesus taught a new way of living that threatened the established systems of religion and politics, drawing anger from many. When facing people's anger, he stayed assertive and didn't let their strong emotions sway his responses.

- In Luke 10:38–42, Jesus and his disciples were visiting their friends Mary and Martha. While Martha busied herself as hostess, her sister Mary sat with the disciples listening to Jesus teach. The pressure of doing all the preparation got to Martha, so she vented her anger toward Jesus, exclaiming, "Don't you care that my sister has left me to do the work by myself? Tell her to help me!" While Martha's feelings were directed at Mary, she pulled Jesus in to resolve the tension.

  Jesus didn't immediately tell Mary to help Martha. He also didn't tell Martha to either work it out with Mary or forget about it. Jesus gently answered by first validating how Martha felt and then encouraging her to reconsider her priorities: "Martha, Martha, you are worried and upset about many things, but few things are needed—or indeed only one. Mary has chosen what is better, and it will not be taken away from her." Jesus wasn't saying that hospitality was unimportant. Rather, he was patiently helping Martha realize that her anger came from misplaced priorities. Her work mattered, but it was not the "one thing": spending time with Jesus.

  > When facing people's anger, Jesus stayed assertive and didn't let their strong emotions sway his responses.

- Even when anger intensified to violence, Jesus responded assertively. In John 18:10–11, the authorities came to arrest Jesus. One of Jesus' disciples, Peter, desperately swung his sword and cut off a servant's ear. Jesus immediately told Peter, "Put your sword away!" Later, in John 18:19–24, Jesus was brought before the high priest, and an officer struck him unjustly. Jesus challenged the man and the crowd to examine their wrongful motives: "If I said something wrong, testify as to what is wrong. But if I spoke the truth, why did you strike me?"

> Jesus' words and actions in response to anger consistently matched with his values of teaching the truth, loving others, and helping people see their need to change.

Jesus' words and actions in response to anger consistently matched with his values of teaching the truth, loving others, and helping people see their need to change. In doing so, he modeled how we can stay assertive and remain true to our values when facing anger.

5. Jesus Assertively Chose to Be Calm

Throughout his ministry, Jesus found himself in numerous situations where people expressed intense emotions, and he responded by remaining calm and non-anxious.

- In Mark 4:35–41, Jesus was asleep in a boat with his disciples when suddenly there was a great storm. Many of the disciples were experienced fishermen, but they panicked at the intensity of the wind and waves. Out of fear, they woke Jesus, shouting, "Teacher, don't you care if we drown?" Of course, Jesus deeply cared for them, but he didn't respond to their panic with defensiveness or irritation. Instead, he calmed the storm by saying to it, "Quiet! Be still!" Then he addressed the fear that dominated their hearts by patiently asking his disciples, "Why are you so afraid? Do you still have no faith?"

- Luke 12:13–21 shares an incident when a person in a crowd demanded that Jesus decide in his favor concerning a family dispute over inheritance. Jesus didn't allow the man's forceful insistence to affect him, instead assertively refusing to pass judgment and shifting to the real issue of excessive focus on material wealth. Jesus addressed the entire crowd, cautioning them, "Watch out! Be on your guard against all kinds of greed; life does not consist in an abundance of possessions." Through his assertive response to a highly charged situation, Jesus offered an important lesson to everyone in attendance.

> When we assertively choose to be a calm, non-anxious presence, we can help ourselves and others.

Whether it's fear in a crisis, uncertainty with a major decision, pressure to act rashly in an urgent matter, or something else, people's intense emotions can raise our anxiety and make it more likely that we will respond in non-assertive ways. When we assertively choose to be a calm, non-anxious presence, we can help ourselves and others move forward in a healthy manner.

6. Jesus Assertively Expressed and Received Affection

Jesus knew it was important to express his affection for the people he loved and ministered to, and he also valued the affection he received from others.

PART 3: A FAITH PERSPECTIVE ON ASSERTIVENESS

- In John 1:47, when Jesus first met one of his disciples, Nathanael, he greeted him by saying, "Here truly is an Israelite in whom there is no deceit." Jesus used this blessing from a psalm to compliment Nathanael's character and warmly welcome and honor him.

- Jesus told his disciples in John 15:9–15, "As the Father has loved me, so have I loved you. Now remain in my love." Later, he said, "I have called you friends, for everything that I learned from my Father I have made known to you." In that time, a teacher calling his disciples friends was a significant honor. Jesus didn't hold back in expressing the depth of his love and care for those close to him.

> Every person has an intrinsic need to feel loved and valued, and Jesus made sure to express his affection to others.

Every person has an intrinsic need to feel loved and valued, and Jesus made sure to express his affection to others. He was also open to receiving affection, acknowledging the love others had for him.

- When Jesus shared a meal with a number of his disciples and friends, as described in Matthew 26:6–13, Mary wanted to express her gratitude to Jesus for all he had done. So, she took some expensive perfume and poured it on Jesus' head. Jesus' disciples responded in a judgmental way, saying the perfume should have been sold and the money used for charity. But Jesus assertively countered the disciples, saying, "Why are you bothering this woman? She has done a beautiful thing to me." By defending Mary's actions, Jesus made clear that he accepted and appreciated her expression of affection.

7. Jesus Assertively Drew Appropriate Boundaries

Jesus loved all and sought to serve people everywhere. Even so, he established appropriate boundaries when he needed to care for himself, when he was being pressured to stray from his principles, or when others were aiming to manipulate him.

- Over the course of Jesus' ministry, more and more people gathered to hear him and ask for help. In circumstances like that, surrounded by unending needs, it would be easy to feel pressured to keep working to the point of burnout or giving up. But Jesus knew it was okay, even necessary, to stop and rest. Luke 5:15–16 shows how he "often withdrew to lonely places and prayed," taking time to recharge so he could best continue his ministry of serving others.

- With his fame growing, people began pressuring Jesus to take over as their political leader, hoping he would overthrow the oppressive Roman government. But that was not what Jesus had come to do—he intended to make a more lasting change in how people loved one another and related to God. In John 6:14–15, when he saw that the crowd intended to make him their king by force to stand against the Romans, he didn't passively go along or aggressively shout them down. Instead, he assertively set a boundary by withdrawing to a mountain alone so he wouldn't be coerced to stray from his real purpose.

> Boundaries are every bit as important for us as for Jesus.

Boundaries are every bit as important for us as for Jesus. We can establish and maintain boundaries in our lives by being aware of our limitations, watching for demands that would compromise our principles, and distancing ourselves from certain volatile situations as necessary.

At Times Jesus Assertively Chose to Act in an Aggressive or Passive Way

Jesus was always assertive. His words and actions were never incongruent with his character and purpose. The ways Jesus responded in different circumstances may have varied, but his approach was always aligned with his mission and ministry. This included situations where he *chose* to act aggressively or passively.

Jesus Assertively Chose to Act Aggressively

When Jesus chose to take aggressive actions, he remained in control of his emotions. He was intentional and purposeful in that decision.

- Sometimes this involved strong words, as in Matthew 23:1–36, when Jesus spoke out against the religious leaders of the time. He called them "hypocrites" for making strict rules they didn't keep in their own hearts, as well as "blind guides" for leading people astray from how God intended them to live. He compared them to "whitewashed tombs," appearing pristine from the outside but full of death inside. These strong words were necessary to point out the destructiveness of these leaders' actions. Jesus grieved the spiritual harm their broken system was causing, and his heart went out to the marginalized people who suffered under it. He deliberately spoke harshly to get the leaders' attention, hoping they would turn from their wrongful ways, and to alert the people of the danger they faced.

- Jesus also chose to act aggressively when he visited the temple in Jerusalem, depicted in Mark 11:15–17. In Jesus' day, there was a designated worship area for those who weren't Jewish, but that area had instead been set up like a marketplace. The sacred space had become commercialized. Jesus was rightly angry at the people doing business there because it obstructed others' ability to pray and worship. He chose to act urgently for the spiritual health of others and to restore the sanctity of the temple, deciding that an impactful, no-nonsense response was needed.

  Seeing that need, "Jesus entered the temple courts and began driving out those who were buying and selling there. He overturned the tables of the money changers and the benches of those selling doves, and would not allow anyone to carry merchandise through the temple courts." In doing so, Jesus made a powerful statement and restored that space for the worshippers.

  > Jesus was not motivated by self-interest when he chose to act in an aggressive way.

It's important to note that Jesus was not motivated by self-interest when he chose to act in an aggressive way. At all times, his motivation was love and care for others.

Jesus Assertively Chose to Act Passively

There were times when Jesus intentionally acted passively. His passive actions did not come out of insecurity, fear, or indecision; the actions were deliberate and focused on what would best serve people.

PART 3: A FAITH PERSPECTIVE ON ASSERTIVENESS

Most of Jesus' passive actions were related to his arrest and crucifixion. Jesus knew that in order to complete his mission and reconcile people to God, he needed to die, so he willingly gave himself up for the good of others.

- In Matthew 26:47–56, Jesus didn't challenge the authorities when they unjustifiably arrested him; instead, he simply said, "Do what you came for." When his disciples tried to forcefully intervene, Jesus said, "Do you think I cannot call on my Father, and he will at once put at my disposal more than twelve legions of angels? But how then would the Scriptures be fulfilled that say it must happen in this way?" Jesus chose to passively go to trial.

- During his trial in Luke 23:6–10, Jesus was sent to the corrupt King Herod, who wanted him to do some miracle or stunning act on command. But Jesus remained silent—he wasn't there to perform for someone who wasn't interested in his mission. Even when others accused him and hurled insults at him, Jesus chose not to respond at all.

> Jesus chose to act passively out of love, even to the point of an agonizing death on a cross.

- Soon after, as described in Matthew 27:11–14, Jesus was questioned by the Roman governor Pontius Pilate, who asked him to answer the religious leaders' accusations. Jesus was again silent. He had spent three years teaching the truth and explaining who he was and what he had come to do. There was nothing else for him to say.

Jesus chose to act passively out of love, even to the point of an agonizing death on a cross. As he told his disciples in John

15:13, "Greater love has no one than this: to lay down one's life for one's friends." His ultimate sacrifice in love meant salvation and a new life for those who trust in him.

Jesus communicated with directness, driven by love. He displayed constant and consistent integrity based on his knowledge of God, himself, and his mission. He dedicated his whole life to serving and caring for others, bringing healing to their broken hearts and lives and providing reconciliation to God.

Whatever our situation, Jesus' life provides us with an excellent model for how we can live assertively.

13

From Misunderstanding to Understanding

A man was searching for a religious Christmas card to give to a friend. He noticed a card with a big present on the front and a verse from the book of Revelation, chapter 11: "And those who dwell on the earth will rejoice . . . make merry and send gifts to one another."[1] The verse seemed appropriate, but before sending the card, he decided to read the entire chapter to see what the verse was referring to.

That proved to be the right decision. The verse wasn't referring to Christmas but to a warped celebration after some people attacked two prophets who had taught about God's love and truth—certainly not the message he wanted to send!

This story is just one example of how parts of the Bible can be misunderstood without context. People may think a particular passage sounds like it's saying one thing, but because the full background was left out or certain words misinterpreted, the intended message gets lost.

> Parts of the Bible can be misunderstood without context.

---

1 Revelation 11:10 (NKJV)

FROM MISUNDERSTANDING TO UNDERSTANDING

This chapter addresses five common biblical misunderstandings that relate to assertiveness, looking at the original intent of these teachings.

Self-Worth   *Elevating others above ourselves*

One misconception about the Bible is the belief that it takes a low view of humanity, discouraging people from having a sense of self-worth. Here are a couple of passages that seem to suggest that.

> The Bible teaches that each person has intrinsic worth and deserves respect.

- In Psalm 22:6, King David wrote, "But I am a worm and not a man," despite being a highly respected king.

- The Apostle Paul wrote to the Philippian church in northern Greece, "value others above yourselves, not looking to your own interests but each of you to the interests of the others" (Philippians 2:3–4).

Looking at these and other passages has led some to believe that the Bible views people in a negative light and discourages self-respect. From there, it's easy to assume that the Bible pushes people toward a passive lifestyle of denying one's own needs and wants. But the full context of passages like these tells a different story.

- In Psalm 22, King David called himself a worm because his enemies were mistreating him so badly he felt subhuman. In the psalm, David cried out to God for protection, showing that he believed in his own self-worth enough to stand up for himself and ask God for help. His words were assertive: "Do not be far from

141

me," "Deliver me from the sword," "Rescue me from the mouth of the lions" (Psalm 22:11, 20, 21). David had confidence that his requests would be fulfilled by God. He didn't passively accept abuse from others or believe that he had no value.

- When Paul wrote to the Philippians that people should value others above themselves, he wasn't telling them to think of themselves as unimportant. Rather, he invited them to make deliberate choices to put others first for the sake of the whole community. In his same letter, Paul told his readers not to do anything out of "selfish ambition or vain conceit" (Philippians 2:3). He wrote about Jesus' assertive decision to give up glory and prestige to be a servant to others, seeing it as a model for others to follow.

In addition, many places in the Bible declare how highly God values people.

- Psalm 8:5 says we are "crowned . . . with glory and honor."
- Psalm 139:14 says we are "fearfully and wonderfully made."
- Ephesians 2:10 says, "we are God's handiwork."
- Zephaniah 3:17 says God will rejoice over us with gladness and exult over us with loud singing.

The Bible presents a realistic view of human beings. It doesn't hold back on how people's actions cause brokenness, pain, and discord in the world. Even so, it emphasizes that because God still values us despite the ways we all fall short, we ought to value ourselves and others highly in the same way. The Bible teaches that each person has intrinsic worth and deserves respect, which provides a firm foundation to live assertively.

Turning the Other Cheek

A well-known teaching from Jesus has caused much confusion: "If anyone slaps you on the right cheek, turn to them the other cheek also" (Matthew 5:39).

At first glance, this statement seems to recommend passive behavior, even to the extent of letting another person physically harm you. People have at times misunderstood this as teaching people to accept abuse without consequences. Some even take issue with the entire idea of turning the other cheek, saying it discourages people from standing up for themselves.

But this perspective misses the intent of what Jesus said. At the time, a slap on the right cheek was seen more as a grievous insult than as a physical attack.

> Jesus was not encouraging passive behavior. He was discouraging aggressive retaliation.

Since most people are right handed, slapping someone's right cheek means delivering a backhanded smack, which was perceived as an especially demeaning, calculated attack on another person's dignity.

Jesus knew that most people would respond to such an insult by retaliating, escalating the situation and causing more division and strife. That outcome was the last thing he wanted—as he had said earlier in the same teaching, "Blessed are the peacemakers" (Matthew 5:9). Instead of retaliation, Jesus urged people to turn the other cheek, which required a deliberate response without allowing emotions to take over. It meant standing firm in dignity when the aggressor has attempted to degrade someone's worth through hurtful words or actions.

Jesus was not encouraging passive behavior. He was discouraging aggressive retaliation. Assertively turning the other cheek would keep emotions from escalating, and it could create an opportunity to talk to the person when tensions have calmed down, paving the way to becoming a peacemaker.

Jesus speaks to the value of this kind of reconciliation as well; in the same sermon, he says that if someone has wronged you, before anything else, "First go and be reconciled to them" (Matthew 5:24). Throughout his ministry, he consistently taught assertive principles that would help heal relationships.

It's important not to expand the principle beyond what Jesus intended. It doesn't mean ignoring injustice or denying the need for self-protection. Elsewhere in the Bible, Jesus says that when people cry out in need, God "will see that they get justice" (Luke 18:7–8). He encourages his disciples to be careful and protect themselves when they travel to minister to others (Luke 22:36). He also teaches that it's good to create boundaries with people who intentionally and continually harm us (Matthew 18:15–17).

We can assertively deal with a personal insult without making the situation more heated and still take a stand against unacceptable words and behaviors.

Going the Second Mile

Soon after talking about turning the other cheek, Jesus said, "If anyone forces you to go one mile, go with them two miles" (Matthew 5:41). Many people have heard this teaching used by itself to encourage passive behavior—to simply agree to the demands of others. On the surface, that response may look like giving in or trying to appease those who behave in abusive, manipulative, or exploitative ways. But that's not what Jesus taught.

In Jesus' time, Roman soldiers had the authority to command a Jewish person to transport their luggage from one place to another. Soldiers could approach anyone and tell them to carry their possessions for a mile up the road, and the person would have no choice but to do it. People resented this unfair practice and fulfilled such demands unwillingly and angrily.

Jesus knew that aggression in these circumstances would only cause more conflict, difficulty, or worse. At the same time, a passive response could mean growing resentment and bitterness. However, an assertive response of willingly carrying the soldiers' luggage an extra mile would allow people to take a certain level of control and avoid those negative effects.

By telling people to go another mile beyond what was demanded, Jesus was inviting them to think beyond a momentary inconvenience. They were challenged to turn an oppressive demand into an opportunity to serve another human being. Not long after this teaching, he offered his famous exhortation to "love your enemies" (Matthew 5:44). Jesus instructed his listeners to go the second mile as an exercise in setting aside their self-interest and seeking the good of someone else—even someone who seems like an enemy.

> These might be opportunities to surprise someone with an act of kindness.

That assertive decision to go another mile could also have a powerful effect on the soldier. He might be more sympathetic to the next person he commandeers. He may even be curious about the motives behind that willingness to help, which could open the door to talking about other teachings of Jesus. It's possible for that unexpected gesture to become a positive force in the soldier's life.

We can apply this concept of assertively going the second mile in many situations in life, choosing to go beyond what someone has requested regardless of how assertively or non-assertively that request was made. This may involve responding to requests more positively or offering help with a smile. It just might be an opportunity to surprise someone with an act of kindness.

Meekness

Another well-known but often misunderstood statement from Jesus is "Blessed are the meek, for they will inherit the earth" (Matthew 5:5).

Few words in the Bible are as widely misinterpreted as *meek*. People most often use the word to describe someone as indecisive, easily imposed upon, weak, or lacking in self-respect—in other words, passive and ineffectual. Based on that assumption, it would seem strange that Jesus would say the meek are blessed.

In fact, the original Greek word *praus*, translated as *meek* in the verse, has several additional dimensions that give it much richer meaning. In other writings, the word was used to describe taming a wild animal or a person's capacity for self-control and self-discipline. It gave the image of a person who didn't let malice, bitterness, or other strong emotions rule them. It could also indicate that someone sought the good of others and wasn't governed by pure self-interest or pride. Someone described with the word *praus*, then, was not weak but rather strong and discerning, a person who acted with conviction.

Aristotle defined the word meek *(praus)* as being perfectly situated between becoming too angry (aggressive) and never being angry at all (passive). In other words, being meek is being assertive.[2]

---

2 Aristotle, *Nicomachean Ethics,* trans. Robert C. Bartlett and Susan D. Collins (Chicago: University of Chicago Press, 2011), 37.

Praus can also be translated as *gentle.* Jesus used this sense of the word when he invited people to learn a new way of living: "Take my yoke upon you and learn from me, for I am gentle *(praus)* and humble in heart" (Matthew 11:29). Jesus himself is described as "gentle *(praus)* and riding on a donkey" (Matthew 21:5) as he entered Jerusalem to complete his mission of reconciling people to God. He used his gentleness in assertive and powerful ways.

> Someone described with the word *praus* was not weak but rather strong and discerning, a person who acted with conviction.

Knowing this context, it's easier to see why a meek person would be considered blessed. It's a blessing to be able to maintain control of one's emotions, show displeasure and anger without becoming aggressive, and relate respectfully and kindly without being passive. A person who acts this way can have an extraordinary impact on their own life and those around them, modeling and encouraging others to adopt a better way of relating. As people grow in meekness, they can find greater opportunities for happiness and fulfillment in their relationships.

Eye for Eye, Tooth for Tooth

People are sometimes surprised to learn that the phrase "eye for eye, tooth for tooth" comes from the Bible. It initially appears in the book of Exodus as God instructs the Israelites on the right way to live in relationship with others (Exodus 21:24). On the surface, this phrase may seem to condone aggressive retaliation, and in fact it's often referred to as *Lex Talionis,* Latin for "law of retaliation." A literal interpretation might be, "If you hurt me,

PART 3: A FAITH PERSPECTIVE ON ASSERTIVENESS

I can hurt you right back in the same way"—which seems to conflict with other biblical teachings.

Again, the context matters. In Exodus, "eye for eye, tooth for tooth" is located in a section of laws covering compensation for losses caused by others. Those verses served to establish a code of conduct so no one was taken advantage of and those who were wronged received fair treatment. "Eye for eye, tooth for tooth" set the standard of just and proportionate fines in cases when someone injured another. It was not a warrant for vengeance nor a principle to take literally, but a prescription for equity and an appropriate level of justice.

> Jesus spoke out against aggressive, vengeful attitudes and encouraged working toward reconciliation.

These laws were meant to help curb anger and stop violent pursuits for revenge. At the time, it was common for people to take up matters of justice in their own hands and seek vengeance, with retaliation sparking more retaliation and perpetuating the cycle of violence. But God wanted the Israelite people to live differently and to never let justice exceed what is fair and right.

In Jesus' time, people were misapplying the law, twisting it into a license to seek a certain level of harm in retaliation for injury. It became an encouragement for others to aggressively exercise their right to get even with their enemies—similar to the common misunderstanding of the phrase today.

Jesus spoke out against these aggressive, vengeful attitudes and encouraged working toward reconciliation with those who have done harm. He indicated that people needed to do better than use this statement as justification for revenge. This is where he challenged people to "turn the other cheek" and "go with them two miles."

FROM MISUNDERSTANDING TO UNDERSTANDING

The phrase "eye for eye, tooth for tooth" was never intended to encourage aggressive behavior. Rather, it urged people to examine themselves and make sure they didn't get carried away with their emotions—to seek justice instead of revenge. Jesus wanted people to consider their response and assertively choose love. These kinds of responses pave the way for healing and restoration of relationships.

Contrary to common misunderstandings, the Bible consistently teaches us to live assertively by respecting ourselves and others. Aggressive and passive behavior don't lead to fullness of life, stable relationships with other people, or resolution of conflict. Assertiveness, grounded in respect for ourselves and for others, does.

[Handwritten notes: "Reparation not retaliation" / "You are a beloved child of God. Worthy of + respect"]

14

Relating Assertively to God

Humans are relational beings. Connections with other people are a significant part of our lives and a major way we express our humanity. When we relate assertively, we can more fully enjoy the richness of these connections.

What about relating assertively to God? Some might wonder whether that's appropriate or even possible. But assertiveness is expressing our thoughts, feelings, wants, and needs to someone directly, honestly, and with respect—which is just what God wants from us.

> Assertiveness is expressing our thoughts, feelings, wants, and needs directly, honestly, and with respect—which is just what God wants from us.

The Bible provides guidance on three important questions about relating to God:

- What kind of relationship can we have with God?
- How can we assertively express our feelings to God?
- How can we assertively ask God for help?

This chapter provides an overview of what the Bible says about these questions.

What Kind of Relationship Can We Have with God?

Before exploring how to relate assertively with God, we need to first understand the kind of relationship we can have with God.

The Bible makes it clear that we are always on God's mind. Throughout Scripture, God listens to people and responds to them, offering them a close relationship and calling them friends (Isaiah 41:8). Jesus also calls his disciples friends (John 15:15), and the book of Revelation depicts him seeking the same kind of personal relationship with humanity: "I stand at the door and knock. If anyone hears my voice and opens the door, I will come in and eat with that person, and they with me" (Revelation 3:20).

A mark of a good relationship is when we can comfortably and intimately talk with someone. Several places in the Bible describe people relating to God this way, including how Moses would speak to God face to face "as one speaks to a friend" (Exodus 33:11).

Austin Phelps, a 19th-century theologian, said:

> God is here, within these walls; before me, behind me, on my right hand, on my left hand. . . . I may pour forth my desires before Him, and not one syllable from my lips shall escape His ear. I may speak to Him as I would to the dearest friend I have on earth.[1]

---

[1] Austin Phelps, *The Still Hour: Or, Communion with God* (Boston: D Lothrop Company, 1893), 77–78.

PART 3: A FAITH PERSPECTIVE ON ASSERTIVENESS

God wants to have a deep relationship with each of us. Much like in our human relationships, those who relate to God assertively will experience a deeper connection. This means:

1. **We can be honest about our thoughts and feelings.** God listens without bias, misunderstanding, or impatience. We can share without holding back—God is big enough to handle our difficult emotions, guilt, failings, doubts, or whatever else is on our heart.

2. **We can acknowledge our limitations.** There's no need for us to be embarrassed or fearful about admitting our need for help. Since God is infinitely strong and unbound by human limitations, we can be confident in turning to God.

3. **We can talk with God whenever and wherever.** We don't have to wait for a particular day or until we're in a church or some other holy place. We can choose to communicate to God at any moment.

4. **We can be certain we will be heard and loved.** Each of us is a unique human being, created with equal value and deserving of love. God views us all in this high regard and delights in listening to and caring for us.

Knowing all this, we can feel comfortable relating assertively to God.

How Can We Assertively Express Our Feelings to God?

The Bible is full of guidance on expressing feelings to God—through historical accounts, examples from Jesus, and teachings from the apostles.

Another place in the Bible that provides direction for expressing feelings is the Psalms. As a collection of hymns to sing together, the Psalms helped shape how the worshiping community could voice their feelings. Even today, the Psalms and other passages can guide us to openly and honestly convey our emotions to God, including joy, sadness, fear, and anger.

Joy

We can experience joy for many reasons: milestone events, fulfilling relationships, accomplishments, the wonder of the world around us, and much more. We can also find joy in our relationship with God and in the ways God is at work in our lives.

> Taking time to express joy to God also helps us seek joyfulness in all aspects of life.

Whatever the reason for joy, God loves to hear about it.

As the source of all that is good, God is foundational to any reason we might have for joy. This comes up again and again in the Bible. The prophet Isaiah said, "Shout aloud and sing for joy" because God was with his people (Isaiah 12:6). While overseeing the rebuilding of Jerusalem's wall after its destruction, Nehemiah told the people that they could be strengthened in challenging times by the joy of knowing God was with them (Nehemiah 8:10).

Many Psalms talk about the joy that comes from what God has done, each expressing it in their own unique way.

- The psalmist wrote that God's teaching and guidance "are right, giving joy to the heart" (Psalm 19:8).

- After experiencing healing from grief, the psalmist said God "clothed me with joy" (Psalm 30:11).

- In response to God's protection, the psalmist declared, "Let all who take refuge in you be glad; let them ever sing for joy" (Psalm 5:11).
- Reflecting on all God's works, the psalmist wrote, "We are filled with joy" (Psalm 126:3).

There isn't just one way to express joy. What's important is that it comes from the heart.

Sometimes people have misconceptions like the following that may keep them from assertively relating to God with joy and thanksgiving.

- **Misconception: "I need to express my joy eloquently."** What matters is the sentiment behind the words, not the words themselves. One psalm encourages us to give thanksgiving through "a joyful noise" (Psalm 95:2 ESV), and another describes "glad shouts and songs of praise" (Psalm 42:4 ESV). Expressing joy doesn't require intricately crafted words.

- **Misconception: "I don't need to say anything because God already knows I'm joyful."** Even knowing everything in our hearts, God wants to hear us share our joy. Taking time to express joy to God also helps us seek joyfulness in all aspects of life.

So, freely express your joy to God.

Sadness

All of us inevitably suffer from grief, life difficulties, disappointments, and other painful situations at times. Often in these circumstances, we try to keep our sadness inside, to put on a happy face and avoid bothering others with our feelings.

But it's important to talk about these hurts and bring them to the surface in order to start the healing process.

> God wants to hear our sadness.

That's why God wants to hear us share our sadness—and why we can do so assertively. While other individuals might respond to us with platitudes, pile on the pressure to be positive or strong, or rush to give advice, God listens with patience and love.

The Psalms include numerous examples of people expressing sadness.

- **When feeling attacked:** "How long must I wrestle with my thoughts and day after day have sorrow in my heart? How long will my enemy triumph over me?" (Psalm 13:2).

- **When feeling betrayed:** "Listen to my prayer, O God, do not ignore my plea; hear me and answer me. My thoughts trouble me and I am distraught because of what my enemy is saying, because of the threats of the wicked" (Psalm 55:1–3a).

- **When feeling isolated, far from home, and deserted by loved ones:** "Hear my voice when I call, Lord; be merciful to me and answer me. . . . Though my father and mother forsake me" (Psalm 27:7, 10a).

- **When grieving a loss:** "Have mercy on me, Lord, for I am faint; heal me, Lord, for my bones are in agony. . . . I am worn out from my groaning. All night long I flood my bed with weeping and drench my couch with tears. My eyes grow weak with sorrow" (Psalm 6:2, 6–7a).

The Psalms are full of people who cried out to God in their sadness, asking how long their grief would last. They were direct and honest about their feelings, assertively sharing their pain and disappointment with God.

We may at times hold back from expressing sadness to God, assuming that God isn't listening, doesn't care, or will grow impatient with our complaints. But God willingly listens to and accepts any sadness we might need to express. One of the psalmists wrote, "I cry aloud to God . . . and he will hear me" (Psalm 77:1 ESV). Another said to God, "You have kept count of my tossings; put my tears in your bottle. Are they not in your book?" (Psalm 56:8 ESV)

The story of the prophet Elijah illustrates how God responds when we're honest about our sadness. Elijah had upset Jezebel, the queen of Israel, so much that she ordered his execution. Despondent, Elijah fled to the wilderness, and in the depths of depression he told God, "I have had enough, LORD. . . . take my life." God responded by providing food for him. Later, when Elijah hid in a cave, God asked what he was doing there. Elijah said he felt completely alone and miserable, his life on the line for doing the right thing. God reassured Elijah that he wasn't alone and guided him toward those who would help his ministry (1 Kings 19:1–18).

> When we suffer, we can assertively tell God about it and trust God to listen and respond.

When we suffer, we can assertively tell God about our sadness and trust God to listen and respond.

Fear

People handle fear in different ways. Some try to bury the feelings and pretend they don't exist. Others may open up a little to someone but hold back so as not to appear weak.

But we can express our fear to God without worry of judgment. When King Hezekiah faced an invading Assyrian force that had massacred countless people and now stood outside the walls of Jerusalem, he feared that all was lost. Hezekiah went to the sanctuary of God, spread out a threatening letter from the invading army's general, and prayed:

> We can express our fear to God without worry of judgment.

> Give ear, LORD, and hear; open your eyes, LORD, and see; listen to all the words [the general] has sent to ridicule the living God. It is true, LORD, that the Assyrian kings have laid waste all these peoples and their lands. . . . Now, LORD our God, deliver us from his hand. . . . (Isaiah 37:17–18, 20).

Hezekiah wasn't ashamed or worried God would see him as weak. He assertively went to God with his fear.

Whether we are overwhelmed, anxious, or scared, we too can approach God directly about our fear. Here's how some of the psalmists did this:

- "Keep me safe, my God, for in you I take refuge" (Psalm 16:1).

- "When I am afraid, I put my trust in you. In God, whose word I praise—in God I trust and am not afraid" (Psalm 56:3–4).

- "Listen to my prayer, O God, do not ignore my plea; hear me and answer me. . . . My heart is in anguish within me; the terrors of death have fallen on me. Fear and trembling have beset me; horror has overwhelmed me" (Psalm 55:1, 4–5).

PART 3: A FAITH PERSPECTIVE ON ASSERTIVENESS

Other psalmists wrote of how God listened and responded to their fear:

- **When afflicted with physical and financial turmoil:** "I sought the Lord, and he answered me; he delivered me from all my fears" (Psalm 34:4).

- **When surrounded by danger:** "The Lord is with me; I will not be afraid. What can mere mortals do to me?" (Psalm 118:6).

- **When fearful for health and safety:** "Whoever dwells in the shelter of the Most High will rest in the shadow of the Almighty. . . . You will not fear the terror of night, nor the arrow that flies by day, nor the pestilence that stalks in the darkness, nor the plague that destroys at midday" (Psalm 91:1, 5–6).

As the early church faced growing pressure to abandon their faith to avoid persecution, the Apostle Peter wrote to calm their fears: "Cast all your anxiety on [God] because he cares for you" (1 Peter 5:7). Peter encouraged them to boldly give their fears and worries to God, who would gladly take on those burdens for their sake.

We are invited to spread out our fears like King Hezekiah's letter before God. When we get our fears out in the open to God, we open ourselves up to relief and comfort. Perhaps the most well-known Psalm illustrates this best:

The Lord is my shepherd, I lack nothing.
    He makes me lie down in green pastures,
he leads me beside quiet waters,
    he refreshes my soul.
He guides me along the right paths
    for his name's sake.

Even though I walk
>through the darkest valley,
I will fear no evil,
>for you are with me (Psalm 23:1–4a).

Anger

Out of all the emotions, anger might be the most challenging to express assertively to God. Many have been taught that it's wrong to be angry, especially when relating to God. They may worry about offending God or making matters worse.

There's nothing at all wrong with being angry when relating to God. People may have limits when it comes to handling expressions of strong emotions, but God does not.

> There's nothing at all wrong with being angry when relating to God.

The Psalms offer an excellent guide for handling anger, speaking directly about it with the understanding that God can accept it:

- **When life doesn't make sense:** "Why, LORD, do you stand far off? Why do you hide yourself in times of trouble?" (Psalm 10:1).

- **Amid numerous hardships:** "LORD, do not forsake me; do not be far from me, my God. Come quickly to help me, my Lord and my Savior" (Psalm 38:21–22).

- **When the strong prey on the weak:** "O God, why have you rejected us forever? Why does your anger smolder against the sheep of your pasture? . . . We are given no signs from God . . . and none of us knows how long this will be" (Psalm 74:1, 9).

PART 3: A FAITH PERSPECTIVE ON ASSERTIVENESS

- **When difficulties seem unchanging:** "Awake, Lord! Why do you sleep? Rouse yourself! Do not reject us forever. Why do you hide your face and forget our misery and oppression?" (Psalm 44:23–24).

The psalmists spoke directly to God about their anger and their reasons for it because they knew God could handle their questions and emotions. God doesn't respond to anger by recoiling, withdrawing, or getting angry in return. That's why the psalmists felt safe complaining and protesting, confident that God would listen and respond. Nothing we can say will diminish God's love.

Two points in chapter 9 can also help with assertively expressing anger to God.

> The psalmists felt safe complaining and protesting, confident that God would listen and respond.

- **Be clear, direct, and honest.** Because we're sharing with someone who loves and cares for us, we can express our anger openly. We don't have to conceal our true feelings or beat around the bush.

- **Listen for God's response.** God may not respond right away or in the way we expect. However, pouring out angry feelings to God can often bring a sense of peace, reassurance, and awareness of God's presence. For example, after expressing challenging emotions, one psalmist wrote, "You, Lord, hear the desire of the afflicted; you encourage them, and you listen to their cry, defending the fatherless and the oppressed" (Psalm 10:17–18a). Another concluded, "Lord, I wait for you; you will answer, Lord my God" (Psalm 38:15).

One more note: At times a psalm will express anger or some other strong emotion in one verse and then shift to a tone of hope and encouragement a few lines later. This doesn't mean the writer immediately moved past their anger and changed their perspective; they may have wrestled with their emotions for a long time between those lines. As one biblical scholar noted, "It sometimes appears that the psalmist changed his negative feelings to positive ones in a brief moment, but this isn't how it happened. The Psalms compress time in such a way that what was a long process appears as a sudden insight."[2] With time, anger can give way to God's peace.

> Whatever emotion we have, we can go to God to assertively say what is on our heart at any time and any place.

Whatever emotion we have, we can go to God to assertively say what is on our heart at any time and any place. God will meet us there to patiently and lovingly listen and care.

How Can We Assertively Ask God for Help?

As chapter 8 mentioned, asking someone for help can feel like a challenge—whether because of embarrassment, worries about appearing pushy or needy, or some other reason. But none of those challenges apply when it comes to asking God for help. God will always gladly hear and answer our requests in whatever way is best for us, even if it's not always clear how at the time.

---

2 Tremper Longman III, *How to Read the Psalms* (Downers Grove, IL: InterVarsity Press, 1988), 81.

Jesus used this analogy to make that point: "Which of you, if your son asks for bread, will give him a stone? Or if he asks for a fish, will give him a snake?" (Matthew 7:9–10). Jesus goes on to make the point that if even imperfect human beings can answer requests in an appropriate way, God will do even more to address our deepest needs.

The Bible regularly describes how God responds to calls for help:

- **When seeking wisdom:** ". . . ask God, who gives generously to all without finding fault, and it will be given to you" (James 1:5).

- **When requesting relief from anxiety:** "Do not be anxious about anything, but in every situation, by prayer and petition, with thanksgiving, present your requests to God. And the peace of God, which transcends all understanding, will guard your hearts and your minds in Christ Jesus" (Philippians 4:6–7).

- **When praying for protection from danger:** "I lift up my eyes to the mountains—where does my help come from? My help comes from the Lord, the Maker of heaven and earth. . . . The Lord will keep you from all harm—he will watch over your life; the Lord will watch over your coming and going both now and forevermore" (Psalm 121:1–2, 7–8).

- **When asking for justice in the midst of oppression:** "And will not God bring justice for his chosen ones, who cry out to him day and night?" (Luke 18:7).

> We don't have to be shy about asking God for help. God knows our needs and doesn't begrudge our requests.

Jesus gave an invaluable model for assertively requesting help from God: the Lord's Prayer in Matthew 6:9–13.

The prayer starts with praise . . .

> *"Our Father in heaven,*
> *hallowed be your name,"*

and acknowledges God's power . . .

> *"Your kingdom come, your will be done,*
> *on earth as it is in heaven."*

Then it asks God for essential needs . . .

> *"Give us today our daily bread,"*

for inner change and forgiveness . . .

> *"And forgive us our debts,*
> *as we also have forgiven our debtors,"*

and for protection . . .

> *"And lead us not into temptation,*
> *but deliver us from the evil one."*

Whatever our specific needs may be, this prayer offers a great template for bringing them to God.

Here are some additional ideas, drawn from chapter 8, that can make it easier to approach God with requests for help:

- **Determine specific types of help you need.** Think through what you are asking for and why. Gather your thoughts and consider your situation at a deeper level so you can ask for what you truly need.

- **Clearly communicate your needs.** Sometimes people feel reluctant to make specific requests of God, but it's best to articulate exactly what you need. God's response may surprise you.

PART 3: A FAITH PERSPECTIVE ON ASSERTIVENESS

- **Identify ways God has helped in the past.** Doing this can help you approach your requests with a hopeful, expectant frame of mind and can serve as a helpful reminder of God's grace.

We don't have to be shy about asking God for help. God knows our needs and doesn't begrudge our requests. We can be assertive when asking for what we need, trusting in God's love for us.

Humans are meant to be in relationships, including a relationship with God. The love, peace, patience, forgiveness, and joy that come from relating assertively to God can be deeply satisfying and life-transforming.

PART 4

Taking Assertiveness to the Next Level

15

Assertive Listening

When someone else is talking, people are often so focused on what they want to say in response that they aren't really listening. That can result in a serious disconnect in the conversation and prevent good relating. To respond assertively, you need to hear and understand what the other person is saying.

How well you listen will have a major impact on how well you communicate. Assertive listening brings a number of benefits to both you and the other person.

- It helps you learn about the situation at hand, gathering all the pertinent facts and details.

- It helps you see things from the other person's perspective and more fully understand what they're thinking and feeling.

- It may in turn help them more clearly understand their own thoughts and feelings. As you encourage them to share, they have the opportunity to listen to themselves and may gain new insights into their own experience.

PART 4: TAKING ASSERTIVENESS TO THE NEXT LEVEL

- It communicates care and respect. By putting forth the time and effort to truly listen, you show the person that you value them and what they have to say. That builds trust and can strengthen the relationship.

- It helps create a calm, non-anxious environment. When you listen in a patient and relaxed manner, you help others relax as well. That will help both of you remain composed and objectively talk through the issue at hand.

- It encourages the other person to listen assertively to you, paving the way for much more effective dialogue where you both seek a shared understanding.

Here are some principles for listening assertively.

Listen Intently

Stay intently focused on what the other person is saying. You want to leave no doubt that you are genuinely paying close attention.

Your body language is crucial here. The guidelines in chapter 5 apply—keep your posture and position similar to the other person's and maintain comfortable eye contact without staring or shifting your gaze constantly. It can also help to nod at appropriate times to show that you're following along. Show your attentiveness in a way that feels natural and authentic to you.

When you listen intently, you won't have to say, "I'm listening to you"—the other person will be able to tell through your eyes, expression, and body language.

> Show your attentiveness in a way that feels natural and authentic to you.

ASSERTIVE LISTENING

Listen without Interrupting   *Don't interrupt*

At certain points while the person is talking, you might feel tempted to jump in with your own thoughts or opinions, possibly to refute what they said, urge them to reconsider, or defend your own point of view. If so,

> You'll have a chance to respond later. For now, it's their turn to talk.

catch yourself before you say anything. Interrupting can create an unsafe atmosphere where the other person has the impression that you aren't really interested in what they have to say. Instead, do your best to <u>set aside your own thoughts</u> and stay focused on listening, allowing the person to say fully what's on their mind. You'll have a chance to respond later. For now, it's their turn to talk.

Listen to Learn

The goal of your listening is to learn as thoroughly and accurately as possible what the other person is thinking and feeling. This allows you to join your understanding of the situation with theirs, resulting in a more complete picture for both of you.

> Let the other person do most of the talking while you process what they share.

When you're listening assertively, you'll let the other person do most of the talking while you process what they share. This doesn't mean you'll be totally silent; from time to time, you might give verbal cues to indicate you're listening or ask questions to clarify details or fill in any gaps.

It can also be helpful to check the accuracy of your understanding by <u>reflecting back</u> what you've heard, summarizing in

PART 4: TAKING ASSERTIVENESS TO THE NEXT LEVEL

your own words what you think the person said. The person can then confirm your understanding or offer clarification.

Once you've gathered the relevant information and gained a sense of the other person's views on the matter, you'll be in a much better position to respond in an assertive way.

Listen through Any Discomfort

At times, listening to someone may bring some discomfort. For example:

- The person might express difficult feelings that are painful to hear, possibly even directed toward you.

- The person might see the situation differently from you and express thoughts, opinions, or ideas contrary to what you think.

- The person might say something that not only challenges your own view of the situation but also contains at least some element of truth, making it even harder for you to acknowledge.

In times like these, the discomfort can make it easy to stop listening, tune the person out, react defensively, argue with the other person, or try to deny what they're saying. Letting uncomfortable feelings control your response, though, will get in the way of assertiveness and likely increase others' discomfort as well.

> As much as possible, listen through any discomfort and remain a calm presence.

So, as much as possible, listen through any discomfort and remain a calm presence. Be aware of what you're feeling, but keep your attention on what is being said. Most likely, you will become less anxious as you listen and gain a more complete understanding, and your reduced anxiety can help the other person feel more comfortable as well.

Respond—and Then Be Ready to Listen Again

After the other person has fully expressed themselves, depending on the context and direction of the conversation, it might be appropriate or necessary for you to respond. That may involve providing more information, asking for clarification, offering an explanation, presenting an alternative, expressing empathy, or replying in some other way. In whatever way you do respond, remain assertive in what you say.

Then, once you're done talking, be ready to listen some more. You might even ask, "What do you think about that?" The person won't always have more to add, but they might have some thoughts to share about what you just said. In any case, your willingness to continue listening helps the conversation remain assertive and invites the best sharing for all involved.

> Your willingness to continue listening helps the conversation remain assertive and invites the best sharing for all involved.

Good listening is crucial to assertiveness. It helps you and the other person make a connection based on trust, respect, and a shared commitment to learning from one another, opening the door to better communication. Although assertively listening doesn't guarantee that you'll find common ground, it does establish a solid foundation for understanding each other and finding the most positive outcome.

16

Assertiveness in Challenging Situations

The vast majority of the time, coming up with an assertive response is pretty straightforward. It may take some effort, but with time and practice you can quickly identify what to say and do in a given situation.

Occasionally, however, you'll run into more challenging situations—issues that require a bit more thought and possibly some planning. Maybe conflict (or the potential for conflict) is involved, emotions are strong, the stakes are high, or it's a circumstance where you personally find it difficult not to respond passively or aggressively.

Here are three examples of challenging situations:

Reggie was reaching his limit with his roommate Zach's art hobby. It hadn't been a problem at first—Zach kept it largely contained to his room, and Reggie had to admit Zach had a knack for painting. But over time, Zach's workspace started to encroach more and more on their shared living area, forcing Reggie to step over and around art supplies and move paintings out of the way. Most irritating of all,

Zach cleaned his brushes in the kitchen sink and often left streaks of paint all over the basin. Whenever Reggie tried to bring up the issue, Zach would respond defensively, as if Reggie were trying to stifle his creativity. Reggie didn't want their friendship to fall apart, but he knew something had to change soon.

Mila fumed as she left the weekly staff meeting. Two weeks ago, she'd had a project brainstorming session with Toni to bounce some ideas off each other. When they'd gone into their staff meeting the next day, Toni had brought up one of Mila's ideas before Mila could mention it herself and then didn't acknowledge where it had come from. Others on the team, not knowing it was originally Mila's idea, praised Toni for her suggestion. Worried about seeming petty or desperate for attention, Mila had let it slide at the time. But then, at the next staff meeting, the same thing happened again. And now today, Toni had jumped in with yet another of Mila's ideas and accepted all the credit for it. Mila had enough. She knew she needed to say something to Toni, but she also wanted to say it in a way that both got her point across and maintained a productive working relationship.

Daniel had been actively involved in theater throughout high school and college, so he was thrilled when his daughter got a part in a community play. He went with her to the first cast and crew meeting and started chatting with some of the others there, reminiscing about the productions he'd acted in or directed. During the meeting, the director mentioned that she was looking for someone to help out at rehearsals and sub if she couldn't make it. To Daniel's dismay, one of the people he'd been chatting with immediately said, "Daniel has all kinds of experience! He'd be great!" After the meeting, the director came up to Daniel to see whether he'd be willing to help out, emphasizing that she was stretched thin and could really use his assistance. Although Daniel sympathized with her, he had just launched a small business, leaving him no time to add another commitment to his busy work and family schedule. Still, he felt guilty saying no. . . .

An excellent tool for assertively communicating what you want in a challenging situation is the *DESC approach,* a technique developed by Sharon and Gordon Bower.[1] The acronym DESC outlines a four-step method to help you plan for and deliver an assertive message.

THE DESC APPROACH
BEING ASSERTIVE IN CHALLENGING SITUATIONS

D — **DESCRIBE THE SITUATION**

E — **EXPRESS YOUR FEELINGS ABOUT THE SITUATION**

S — **SPECIFY WHAT YOU WANT**

C — **DESCRIBE THE CONSEQUENCES ASSOCIATED WITH YOUR REQUEST**

---

1 Sharon Anthony Bower and Gordon H. Bower, *Asserting Yourself: A Practical Guide for Positive Change,* updated edition (Boston: Da Capo Lifelong Books, 2004).

ASSERTIVENESS IN CHALLENGING SITUATIONS

1. ***D**escribe* **the Situation.** Explain to the other person your observations of the situation as well as actions or behaviors that you believe need to be addressed.

2. ***E**xpress* **Your Feelings about the Situation.** Let the person know how the situation is affecting you personally by describing the feelings you're experiencing as a result.

3. ***S**pecify* **What You Want.** Clearly state what you want the person to do to resolve the situation.

4. **Describe the *C*onsequences.** Tell the person what will happen as a result of their doing—or not doing—what you want them to do.

When you're confronted with a difficult situation, these four steps can help you respond in the most effective, assertive way. Although you may need to intentionally think through each step the first few times you use the DESC approach, as you become more familiar with the process you'll be better able to respond more quickly and with less advance planning.

Let's take a deeper look at the DESC steps and how Reggie, Mila, and Daniel could apply them.

Describe the Situation

D First, explain how the situation appears from your perspective, objectively describing what you see, hear, and experience. Stick to the facts of the situation as much as you can without adding in your own interpretation or assumptions.

Reggie: *"Zach, I know how important painting is to you. But lately you've been leaving your art supplies all over the living* room. Also, there's usually paint streaks in the kitchen sink after you clean your brushes."

Mila: "The last few staff meetings, you shared ideas that I came up with in our brainstorming sessions, but you didn't mention those ideas were originally mine."

Daniel: "I know you're feeling overwhelmed with the play, and I'm sure having an assistant would be a big help. I'm really not in a position to take on something like that, though."

In all three scenarios, the person objectively described the situation without yet getting into their feelings. Beginning with a fact-based description helps start the conversation on a neutral, less emotionally charged track.

E *Express* Your Feelings about the Situation

Speak personally about what feelings the situation has brought up in you. Own the feelings, use *I* messages, and avoid implying the other person makes you feel the way you do.

Reggie: "I'm annoyed that I have to pick up the supplies around the living room and clean up the sink."

Mila: "I'm upset that I haven't had the chance to share my own ideas and that you haven't given me credit for them with the group."

Daniel: *"I feel awkward that someone volunteered me, and I feel bad that you got your hopes up."*

Each person described the feelings they were experiencing because of the situation but refrained from making accusations and inviting a defensive response.

S *Specify* What You Want

Ask for what you want, and ask specifically. That's a key for any assertive communication, but a challenging situation amplifies the importance of being clear and direct about what you want. Keep your requests manageable and reasonable, ideally only one or two at a time.

Reggie: *"I'd like you to put away your supplies and clean up the sink when you're done painting."*

Mila: *"During staff meetings, I'd appreciate if you would give me a chance to present the ideas I came up with."*

Daniel: *"I wish I could help, but I just can't add another thing to my plate, so I have to decline."*

In a very clear manner, all three stated what specifically they wanted to see happen.

PART 4: TAKING ASSERTIVENESS TO THE NEXT LEVEL

C Describe the *Consequences* ~positive~

When possible, describe the positive outcomes associated with the situation. Threats and predictions of dire consequences often lead to defensiveness and anger in listeners. It's easier to reach a positive result by showing the other person how cooperating will be in their best interest as well as yours. If you must specify negative consequences, make sure they're appropriate and something you're willing to carry out.

Reggie: *"Doing that would make the apartment easier to get around in and keep clean."*

Mila: *"I think we make a good team, and I'd like to keep working together. If you make that change, I'll feel more comfortable sharing my ideas with you in the future."*

Daniel: *"I know I wouldn't be able to commit to the role, which wouldn't be fair to you or anyone else. I hope you find someone who can help."*

The three people concluded by explaining potential outcomes for their situations.

Following the DESC model doesn't guarantee that the other person will go along with what you say or that you'll get the results you're hoping for. Whatever happens, though, communicating assertively—clearly, concisely, and directly—gives you the best chance of resolving the situation in a way that avoids additional tension and brings about the best outcome for everyone involved.

17

The Caring Candor Window

The Caring Candor Window is a leadership tool we developed at Stephen Ministries and have been using in our teaching since 2005. It provides a visual way to understand:

- how leaders can most effectively provide feedback, guidance, and support to those they lead; and
- how members of a team can optimally relate to one another while working together to carry out a mission.

Although some of the terminology differs a little from the rest of the book, we're including this concept because the behaviors it describes are applicable to any human relationship, giving you another perspective on what it means to be assertive or non-assertive.

The Caring Candor Window is defined by two axes.

- The up-down axis stands for *directness,* or how clearly and straightforwardly a person shares what's on their mind.
- The left-right axis represents *gentleness,* or how much care, consideration, and respect a person shows when relating to others.

Depending on how high or low a person's directness and gentleness are, they'll fit into one of four panes, each representing a different way of relating.

The Caring Candor Window

Gentleness: High ← → Low
Directness: High ↑ ↓ Low

	High Gentleness	Low Gentleness
High Directness	**1. Caring Candor** — High Directness, High Gentleness	**2. Harsh Clarity** — High Directness, Low Gentleness
Low Directness	**3. Sweet Haziness** — Low Directness, High Gentleness	**4. Harsh Haziness** — Low Directness, Low Gentleness

Copyright © 2005, 2024 by Stephen Ministries. All rights reserved.

1. Caring Candor (High Directness, High Gentleness)

The person communicates with clarity and openness, as well as kindness and respect. They honestly share the truths people need to hear in order to learn, grow, and improve, and they do so motivated by a sincere desire to help people succeed.

2. Harsh Clarity (High Directness, Low Gentleness)

The person speaks clearly and honestly, but does so bluntly, showing little care or respect. Others are likely to perceive the person as hostile, callous, and mean-spirited. Even if the message is constructive and well intended, the delivery is often more hurtful than helpful.

3. Sweet Haziness (Low Directness, High Gentleness)

The person is so concerned about being liked and not upsetting others that they try to avoid saying anything that might be perceived as negative. They may end up hiding certain truths or sugarcoating realities that people need to hear, denying them opportunities to learn, grow, and succeed.

4. Harsh Haziness (Low Directness, Low Gentleness)

The person regularly relates in ways that are both unclear and unkind. Their words and actions come across as overly critical and insensitive, leaving other people hurt or confused. The person's behavior is largely unpredictable, but they will likely blow up at someone at some point in time.

The goal in seeking to be assertive is to consistently relate with caring candor. The reality, though, is that all of us at times can slip into one or more of the other three ways of relating. By picturing these behaviors in the Caring Candor Window, it becomes easier to identify those times, giving us a chance to move back to caring candor instead.

PART 4: TAKING ASSERTIVENESS TO THE NEXT LEVEL

Four Patterns of Relating

Here is a deeper look at each of these four ways of relating, along with comments from people who participated in our research.

1. Caring Candor

Caring candor is assertiveness. When you relate with caring candor, you are relating assertively. So, a good way to strengthen and grow your assertive skills is to focus on communicating with high directness and high gentleness in your interactions with others.

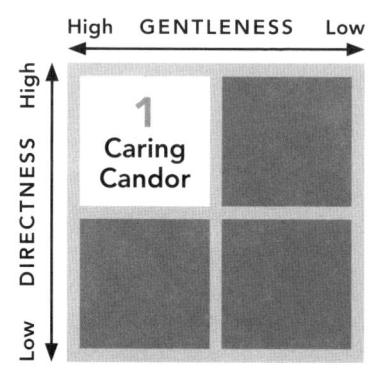

Using caring candor doesn't mean saying only nice, positive things. As appropriate, you'll share critical observations about areas where a person may need to grow, but you'll do so in a concerned, thoughtful way. This approach makes it clear that you care about the person and want to help them learn, grow, and improve, even if your words may sting at first.

A college professor in our research told us:

> "When I look back at times in my life when I've experienced significant growth, it has almost always involved a friend, teacher, colleague, or mentor who was honest and frank in pointing out my deficiencies but did it in a caring, supportive way, seeking to help me correct or overcome them so I could reach my full potential."

2. Harsh Clarity

Harsh clarity, meanwhile, is a form of aggression. It involves relating to others directly and often honestly, but with little care or respect. Someone relating with harsh clarity might mean well—their message may be important and valid—but the aggressive delivery risks negating the value of what they have to say.

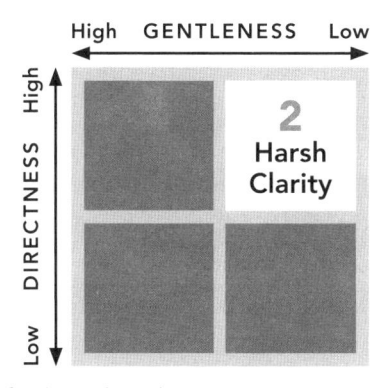

If people tend to react defensively, retreat, or withdraw when you're relaying important information to them, it may be that you're communicating with harsh clarity. It's a good idea to assess your delivery and consider how you can express what you need to say with greater respect, courtesy, and care.

A business executive we talked to shared these thoughts:

*"I place such a high value on being honest and direct with people that I sometimes forget about the gentleness part. Keeping the window concept in mind helps me remember the both-and aspect of the equation. I need to be both direct **and** gentle if I want my feedback to be effective."*

3. Sweet Haziness

Sweet haziness involves being as non-confrontational, amiable, easygoing, and agreeable as possible. Those qualities aren't a problem in and of themselves. When they're used in excess to avoid sharing difficult truths, however, they add up to passive behavior and ineffective communication.

PART 4: TAKING ASSERTIVENESS TO THE NEXT LEVEL

This can be a tempting way to relate. We might see it as caring to spare people's feelings by not being fully open or honest with them about certain problems, weaknesses, or shortcomings. In reality, it's the opposite—it leaves others without the knowledge and understanding they need to grow or improve.

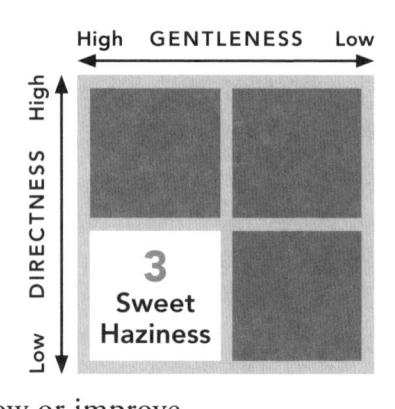

A leader attending one of our training events said this:

> "I wanted to be known as a 'nice boss,' so I'd only say complimentary things to my staff, ignoring or glossing over issues or mistakes. Then our human resources director pulled me aside and said, 'You're not doing your staff any good if you're not being candid with them. You need to point out the negatives too. Otherwise, they won't know when they're doing well or how to grow and do better. If you give criticism sincerely and with care, they'll like and respect you even more.' She was right."

4. Harsh Haziness

Harsh haziness is a very aggressive way to relate. It means communicating with low directness and low gentleness—being critical, unkind, and negative without any explanation or attempt to help someone improve.

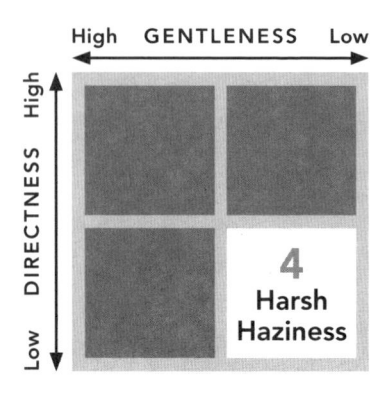

This is typically the most damaging of the non-assertive approaches in the Caring Candor Window. Others will tend to tiptoe around someone who relates in this way, anxious about the risk of setting them off. Harsh haziness instills fear, pushes people away, and damages relationships or prevents them from forming. It can be destructive to teams and individuals alike.

Growing in Caring Candor

The Caring Candor Window can serve as a valuable tool for self-assessment and growth in assertive relating. Periodically, after you've offered feedback or had another interaction that called for assertiveness, ask yourself these questions:

- Which window did I relate in: caring candor, harsh clarity, sweet haziness, or harsh haziness?
- If my relating was low in directness or gentleness, what might be the reasons for that?
- What can I learn from the experience to relate with greater caring candor the next time?

Such self-assessments over time will help you continue to grow your assertiveness skills.

If someone else on your team is relating with harsh clarity, sweet haziness, or harsh haziness, by all means use caring candor to talk with the person about their behavior. In addition, focus on being an example—striving to relate with caring candor, no matter how the person may act in return.

> The more consistently you model assertive behavior, the more likely the person will begin to respond in kind.

The more consistently you model assertive behavior to the person, the more likely they will pick up on your approach and begin to respond in kind.

One final point: As emphasized throughout the book, none of us is perfectly assertive. All of us will occasionally slip into non-assertive patterns of relating. When you do, relate to yourself with caring candor—directly acknowledge where you may have fallen short, while also treating yourself with care, forgiveness, encouragement, and respect.

18

Continuing the Journey

The beginning of this book described how becoming more assertive involves learning a new set of skills. You may have already begun applying or strengthening these skills to relate in better, more effective ways. But even though you've reached the final chapter, your journey will continue with many opportunities ahead.

This chapter gives some final suggestions for how you can keep moving forward in your assertiveness journey.

Identify and Emulate Assertive Models

Most people have one or more individuals in their lives who consistently demonstrate assertive behavior. Perhaps you have a coworker who knows how to share critical feedback in a relaxed and empowering way, a relative who remains composed and respectful when working through a disagreement, or a friend who offers sincere compliments and expresses gratitude and appreciation with ease.

PART 4: TAKING ASSERTIVENESS TO THE NEXT LEVEL

Bctni ✱

After identifying those assertive models, take note of their confidence and poise, observe their words and actions, and learn from them.

Know How You Tend to Respond

Recognizing common situations in which you typically react in non-assertive ways—passively or aggressively—can help you change the way you respond when those same situations arise in the future. Think through what you tend to feel, say, and do in those scenarios you encounter frequently.

- What feelings bubble up inside of you?
- What do you typically say or do—or not say or do?
- What situations are harder for you to act assertively in?
- What types of relationships or people do you find it harder to be assertive with?

> Catching yourself before you react in a non-assertive way empowers you to respond assertively instead.

- If your response in certain circumstances is typically passive or aggressive, what would be an assertive way to respond instead?

Knowing what you usually do in these situations can help you catch yourself before you react in a non-assertive way, empowering you to respond assertively instead.

Continuing the Journey

Practice as Necessary

Occasionally, you may know in advance you'll be having a challenging conversation where the stakes are high and you feel anxious about what to say and do. Practicing for this kind of assertive interaction can be extremely beneficial. Here are suggestions for how you might prepare:

- Write out a script of the assertive message you want to deliver. Think carefully about the purpose and goal for your communication so your script covers all the key points. You can't predict exactly how the conversation will unfold or how the person will respond, but the act of preparing will help you stay focused and on target.

- Practice out loud. Hearing yourself say the words you've written will help you refine them, keep them ingrained in your mind, and build your confidence for speaking them later.

- Rehearse the situation with a trustworthy friend to get feedback. You can practice what you intend to say, get input and advice, and try different ways of responding, which will help you feel much more prepared for the actual conversation.

Stay the Course

Keep in mind that you can't control what others do—only what you do. Even when you're assertive with them, they may not respond in the way you hoped they would.

PART 4: TAKING ASSERTIVENESS TO THE NEXT LEVEL

If so, stay the course and continue to be assertive. Resist any temptation to shift into a passive or aggressive mode. Maintain your focus on communicating calmly, firmly, and gently. Your consistent and persistent assertiveness will maximize the possibility of a positive outcome.

Get Help from Other People

Improving the way you relate isn't something you have to work on alone. Since assertiveness involves interacting with other people, it can be helpful to involve others in your journey to become more assertive.

> Since assertiveness involves interacting with other people, it can be helpful to involve others in your journey to become more assertive.

That can be as simple as telling a few trusted family members or friends about the ways you seek to grow. If people know in advance that you're making changes that are important to you, they can provide support and encouragement along the way. You might even find one or two individuals to serve as confidants with whom you can share specific goals, discuss your progress, and seek feedback from time to time.

If you have been reading this book as part of a group or team—with coworkers, classmates, friends, small group members, or others—you may find it helpful to discuss your progress, share about specific experiences, brainstorm ways to improve, and work together to continue growing your assertiveness skills.

Having the support and encouragement of others can make a significant difference.

Evaluate Your Efforts

Virtually every interaction you have with another person will be an opportunity to be assertive. It's helpful to occasionally evaluate specific interactions to see how you're doing. Here are some helpful questions to consider:

- **Was your message clear and concise?** Did you clearly and calmly communicate the point you wanted to make? Did you stay focused and avoid getting sidetracked? Did you share without long-winded explanations, excuses, or apologies?

- **Were your nonverbal cues congruent with your words?** Did you maintain good eye contact, confident posture, and appropriate distance? Did you avoid excessive or distracting hand and body movements?

- **Were you appropriately firm while also being respectful?** Did you honestly and directly communicate your thoughts and feelings while showing concern for the other person's thoughts and feelings? The Caring Candor Window from chapter 17 can help you reflect on how much directness and gentleness you exhibited.

- **Did you remain assertive throughout the interaction?** After expressing your thoughts, did you listen assertively to the person's response? Did you remain calm and collected through the entire conversation?

> Be sure to celebrate your successes—and build on them for the future.

By periodically evaluating your efforts, you can continue to learn and improve as you grow your assertiveness skills.

Celebrate Your Successes!

When learning any new skill, you'll experience successes and failures along the way. Be patient with yourself when your efforts fall short—look at those instances as an opportunity to learn and grow. But also be sure to celebrate your successes. Affirm yourself, take confidence from your accomplishments, and build on them for the future. If you're discussing this book in a group, take time to celebrate one another's successes as well.

As you continue down this road, you'll see greater and greater growth in your assertive relating. So, accept the challenge, relish the changes in your life, give yourself plenty of encouragement, and enjoy the journey!

Acknowledgments

As we mentioned in the introduction, assertiveness was crucial to the writing of this book. We related directly, honestly, and respectfully with many people to develop the best possible resource on the topic. We'd like to thank them for their role in the development process.

Research Participants

In writing this book, we drew on the thoughts, insights, and life experiences of a multitude of people. This included 2,858 individuals who completed surveys, 1,161 who participated in focus groups, and 173 interviewees. The stories, ideas, and personal wisdom they shared reinforced the book's key points and added life and depth to its examples.

Another 414 people read the manuscript and gave feedback on it at various stages throughout its development. These reviewers included teachers, professors, first responders, physicians, nurses, coaches, pastors, accountants, financial advisors, business owners, salespeople, HR directors, CEOs, real estate agents, attorneys, musicians, and engineers—as well as 47 mental health professionals. The insights and perspectives they all offered helped us refine and polish each chapter, resulting in a stronger resource overall.

Stephen Ministries Staff

We also owe a great deal to our colleagues at Stephen Ministries, who put their all into helping take *Caring Assertiveness* to the next level.

ACKNOWLEDGMENTS

Our thanks go out to our staff for reading the manuscript and offering their honest feedback prior to publication. In addition, we'd like to specifically recognize a number of individuals:

- Isaac Akers, Julie Bode, Lori Kem, and Justin Schlueter, who as primary editors helped organize ideas, sharpen concepts, and refine the manuscript.

- David Bales, Nanette Dost, Justin Schlueter, and Janine Ushe, who shared their theological insights and expertise in the development of the chapters in part 3.

- Emily Winkeler, who coordinated our research and organized four rounds of manuscript reviews, along with our research team including Tammy Franklin, Amanda Hand, Karen Klebe, Pamela Montgomery, Tarja Murrell, and Carter Williams.

- Anna Barrett, David Bode, Stephen Glynn, Lydia Grabau, Addie Gramelspacher, Amity Haugk, Missy Towers, and Rachel Wegener, who as secondary editors helped fine-tune key points throughout the book.

- Becky Bogar, Kathy Hollenbeck, and several other staff mentioned previously, who proofread the manuscript before publication.

- Kirk Geno, who designed the cover, developed the layout, typeset the book, and created the interior graphics.

This book would not be what it is without the contributions of everyone at Stephen Ministries.

Our Families

Finally, we want to express our deep appreciation to our families for helping shape us into who we are and providing love and support during the writing of this book and throughout our lives.

All these people had a crucial part to play in making this book a reality—it was a privilege to work with them. It's our hope that *Caring Assertiveness,* the result of our combined efforts, makes a powerful difference in all your relating.

About the Authors

Kenneth C. Haugk, Ph.D., is a pastor and clinical psychologist. He received his Ph.D. in clinical psychology from Washington University and his M.Div. from Concordia Seminary, both in St. Louis. A member of the American Psychological Association, Dr. Haugk maintained a private practice as a clinical psychologist for many years and has taught psychology and leadership at several universities and seminaries.

Dr. Haugk is the founder and Executive Director of Stephen Ministries. Over the years, he has written books and courses on numerous relational and leadership topics, including *Don't Sing Songs to a Heavy Heart, Journeying through Grief, Cancer—Now What?, When and How to Use Mental Health Resources,* and *The Gift of Empathy.* Dr. Haugk's research and other writing has also been published widely in psychological journals and popular periodicals.

Ken lives in St. Louis. He enjoys playing basketball and pickleball, traveling, rooting for the Cardinals, and spending time with his children and grandchildren.

Joel P. Bretscher has been a member of the staff at Stephen Ministries in St. Louis since 1995, having previously trained and served as a Stephen Minister in Phoenix, Arizona.

As Program Director, Joel leads the writing and editing team in the development of books, videos, training materials, courses, and other resources. He is the lead author of the award-winning book *The Gift of Empathy* and the executive editor of the *Stephen Ministry Leader's Manual* and *Stephen Minister Training Manual.* In addition, he presents at conferences and training events, consults with congregations, and serves on the organization's leadership team.

ABOUT THE AUTHORS

A graduate of Valparaiso University in Indiana, Joel was a longtime competitive swimmer and is a member of the university's Athletic Hall of Fame.

Joel and his wife, Della, live in St. Louis, where they regularly spend time with their son, daughter-in-law, and two grandchildren. When possible, they also enjoy traveling to Hamburg, Germany, to visit their daughter and son-in-law.

Robert A. Musser is a senior writer and editor at Stephen Ministries. He is a key member of the program team that has researched and developed many of the organization's books, courses, training materials, and other resources, including *Cancer—Now What?*, *The Gift of Empathy*, the *Stephen Ministry Leader's Manual*, the *Stephen Leader Online Toolkit*, the *Caring Assertiveness Discussion Guide*, and the Stephen Leader Training Course. He is also the editor of the Devotional Edition of *Joy Comes with the Morning* by William M. Kinnaird.

A graduate of Bradley University in Peoria, Illinois, with a degree in English, Robert has served at Stephen Ministries since 2005. In addition to writing and editing, he trains and mentors other writers on staff, develops and processes research materials, and serves on the training course team.

A resident of St. Louis, Robert enjoys spending his free time writing, studying Japanese, and practicing art and animation.

caringassertiveness.org

About the *Caring Assertiveness* Discussion Guide

This companion resource provides the materials you need to lead a group in studying *Caring Assertiveness* together. With thorough guidance for scheduling and planning, questions for each chapter, and closing activities, it will prepare you to make this group study a fulfilling, enlightening experience for everyone involved.

Many different kinds of groups are using the *Discussion Guide* to study the book and grow in assertiveness, including:

- Workplace groups
- Professional development groups
- Leadership and executive teams
- Teachers and school administrators
- Book clubs
- Men's, women's, and couples' groups
- Parenting groups
- Youth and young adult groups
- College organizations
- Volunteer groups
- Service groups and organizations
- Support groups
- Caregiving groups
- Church staff, deacons, and other church groups
- Other types of groups

Whether your group is well practiced in the area of assertiveness or just beginning to use those skills more consistently, your study will help them strengthen and grow their abilities in this essential way of relating.

Visit **caringassertiveness.org/discussion** to learn more.

About the Stephen Ministries Organization

Stephen Ministries is an international not-for-profit Christian educational organization founded in 1975 and based in St. Louis, Missouri. The year 2025 marks Stephen Ministries' 50th anniversary.

The organization is best known for the Stephen Ministry system of lay caregiving, which is used in more than 14,000 congregations and other types of organizations representing over 190 denominations across the United States and Canada, as well as 30 other countries.

In addition, Stephen Ministries publishes books and conducts seminars and courses on a variety of topics, including assertiveness, grief, dealing with cancer, relationship skills, empathy, leadership, conflict resolution, and crisis care.

The following pages highlight examples of the resources and training offered by Stephen Ministries. To learn more, contact us:

Stephen Ministries
2045 Innerbelt Business Center Drive
St. Louis, Missouri 63114-5765
(314) 428-2600
stephenministries.org

About the Stephen Ministry System of Care

Stephen Ministry is a complete system for training and organizing laypeople to provide emotional and spiritual care to hurting people in the congregation and community.

In Stephen Ministry, Stephen Leaders—specially trained lay leaders, staff, and pastors—are equipped to begin and lead this system in their congregation or organization.

Stephen Leaders, in turn, train and supervise a team of lay caregivers, called Stephen Ministers. *Caring Assertiveness* is one of the books used in their training.

Stephen Ministers then provide emotional and spiritual care to people experiencing grief, divorce, job loss, medical crises, unemployment, and other life difficulties. As a result:

- hurting people receive quality care;
- laypeople use their gifts in meaningful ministry;
- pastors and staff no longer bear the entire burden of trying to personally provide all the care that people need; and
- the caregiving capacity of the church or organization is expanded greatly through highly trained volunteers.

Since 1975, more than 80,000 Stephen Leaders have been trained. These leaders have equipped over 600,000 Stephen Ministers, who have cared for millions of people worldwide.

Visit **stephenministries.org/care** for more information.

Other Resources from Stephen Ministries

Journeying through Grief

Journeying through Grief is a set of four short books to give or send to people at four crucial times during the difficult first year after a loved one has died.

- *A Time to Grieve,* sent at three weeks after the loss
- *Experiencing Grief,* sent at three months
- *Finding Hope and Healing,* sent at six months
- *Rebuilding and Remembering,* sent at eleven months

Each book focuses on what the person is likely to be experiencing at that time and provides care, assurance, encouragement, and hope. Individuals are giving the books to grieving friends and relatives, congregations are using them to minister to people in the church and community, and businesses and other organizations are providing them to employees, customers, clients, and associates.

Written in a caring style that meets grieving people where they are, *Journeying through Grief* provides a simple, powerful way to care again and again.

Also available is a *Giver's Guide* with suggestions for giving the books, along with sample letters to personalize and send with them.

Don't Sing Songs to a Heavy Heart
How to Relate to Those Who Are Suffering

There's a challenge we all face in our lives: We want to reach out and help someone who is hurting, but we worry that our words or actions may unintentionally add to their pain.

Don't Sing Songs to a Heavy Heart offers real-world guidance and commonsense suggestions for caring in ways that hurting people welcome, while avoiding pitfalls that can get in the way of care. Forged from author Kenneth Haugk's own experiences, the book also draws on in-depth research with more than 4,200 people who have faced various kinds of suffering.

For anyone who has ever felt helpless in the face of another person's pain, it offers key insights and ideas for what to say and do—and what not to—when people are hurting. Caregivers and suffering people alike have high praise for this warm, insightful resource.

With its compassionate approach and concrete ideas, *Don't Sing Songs to a Heavy Heart* will help you support hurting people when they need it most.

Christian Caregiving—a Way of Life

Christians sometimes wonder, "How can my faith make a difference in my everyday caring and relating?" *Christian Caregiving—a Way of Life* provides an answer by taking a close look at distinctively Christian care and what sets it apart.

Kenneth Haugk uses his background in psychology and pastoral care to explore profound questions about the connection between faith and care. This book identifies ways you can practice true servanthood, confidently use the tools of your faith, and touch the deepest spiritual concerns of others. The invaluable guidance, insights, and encouragement will help you grow as an effective Christian caregiver—while remembering that God is the Curegiver.

Christian Caregiving—a Way of Life is an inspirational guide for improving your care for people throughout your life—family, friends, neighbors, coworkers, customers, and clients.

OTHER RESOURCES FROM STEPHEN MINISTRIES

Cancer—Now What?
Taking Action, Finding Hope, and Navigating the Journey Ahead

Cancer—Now What? is a book to give to people with cancer and their loved ones to help them navigate the medical, emotional, relational, and spiritual challenges they may face. With 74 concise chapters organized into 12 topical parts, people can go directly to whatever chapters address their needs at any given time.

Author Kenneth Haugk drew on all he learned walking alongside his wife, Joan, during her cancer journey. He built on that foundation through research with thousands of survivors, loved ones, and medical professionals. The result is a comprehensive, easy-to-read book covering a wide range of topics for people dealing with cancer.

People who are giving this book to others include friends, relatives, pastors and church staff, oncologists and other medical professionals, business professionals, and many others. A *Giver's Guide* is also available.

Cancer—Now What? provides a meaningful way to offer tangible care and support to people throughout their cancer journey.

OTHER RESOURCES FROM STEPHEN MINISTRIES

The Gift of Empathy
Helping Others Feel Valued, Cared for, and Understood

The Gift of Empathy is a powerful exploration of how to relate in empathetic ways that make a difference in people's lives. It offers a fresh approach to a familiar topic, providing practical insights and real-life examples that equip readers to better understand, connect with, and care for others.

The book defines what empathy is and isn't, describes its benefits, and shows how to overcome obstacles to effective empathizing. It shares wisdom on using empathy in a wide range of relationships—with spouses and significant others, children, parents, siblings, friends, coworkers, and more.

Authors Joel Bretscher and Kenneth Haugk draw on decades of teaching and consulting in the areas of caring and relating, as well as extensive research with thousands of people from all walks of life. This foundation of knowledge and real-life experience makes *The Gift of Empathy* a uniquely valuable resource for anyone who wants to relate with greater care and compassion.

The Gift of Empathy Discussion Guide

Also available is *The Gift of Empathy Discussion Guide,* a companion resource that provides the tools to facilitate an engaging and enriching group study of the book. It includes questions and activities to help a wide variety of groups enhance their empathy skills.

TO ORDER STEPHEN MINISTRIES' RESOURCES

You can order books and resources from Stephen Ministries in two ways:

1) Visit the Stephen Ministries online store at **stephenministries.org/store.**

2) Call Stephen Ministries at **(314) 428-2600** (Monday through Friday, 8:00 A.M.–5:00 P.M. Central Time).

If you have questions or would like additional information about Stephen Ministries' resources, call us to speak to a member of our Customer Service Team.